Your Happy Healthy Pet™

Dachshund

2nd Edition

GET MORE!
Visit www.wiley.com/
go/dachshund

Ann Gordon

Howell
Book House™

Howell Book House
Published by Wiley Publishing, Inc., Hoboken, New Jersey

Library of Congress Cataloging-in-Publication Data:
Gordon, Ann, 1934–
    Dachshund/Ann Gordon.—2nd ed.
        p. cm.—(Your happy healthy pet)
    Includes index.
    ISBN-10: 0-7645-8386-7 (cloth)
    ISBN-13: 978-0-7645-8386-5 (cloth)
    1. Dachshunds. I. Title. II. Series.
    SF429.D25G66   2005
    636.753'8—dc22
                                                2005002068

Printed in the United States of America

10   9   8   7   6   5   4   3   2

2nd Edition

Book design by Melissa Auciello-Brogan
Cover design by Michael J. Freeland
Illustrations in chapter 9 by Shelley Norris and Karl Brandt
Book production by Wiley Publishing, Inc. Composition Services

About the Author

Ann Gordon has been involved with Dachshunds for more than forty-five years. During twenty of those years, she bred and showed standard smooth Dachshunds in confirmation competition under the kennel name of Ravenridge. In 1969, she was licensed by the American Kennel Club to judge Dachshunds and has judged throughout the United States and Canada, and also recently judged the breed in Australia. Over the years, she has had the honor to judge at five of the Dachshund Club of America's National Specialty Shows.

Not long after she became involved in Dachshunds, Ann became a member of the Dachshund Club of America. Over the many years that she has been a member, she has served as second vice president, first vice president, and as a member of the board of directors—a position she currently holds.

Ann is the Dachshund breed columnist for the *AKC Gazette,* and has been writing this column for twenty years.

About Howell Book House

Since 1961, Howell Book House has been America's premier publisher of pet books. We're dedicated to companion animals and the people who love them, and our books reflect that commitment. Our stable of authors—training experts, veterinarians, breeders, and other authorities—is second to none. And we've won more Maxwell Awards from the Dog Writers Association of America than any other publisher.

As we head toward the half-century mark, we're more committed than ever to providing new and innovative books, along with the classics our readers have grown to love. This year, we're launching several exciting new initiatives, including redesigning the Howell Book House logo and revamping our biggest pet series, Your Happy Healthy Pet™, with bold new covers and updated content. From bringing home a new puppy to competing in advanced equestrian events, Howell has the titles that keep animal lovers coming back again and again.

Contents

Shopping List

You'll need to do a bit of stocking up before you bring your new dog or puppy home. Below is a basic list of some must-have supplies. For more detailed information on the selection of each item below, consult chapter 5. For specific guidance on what grooming tools you'll need, review chapter 7.

☐	Food dish	☐	Nail clippers
☐	Water dish	☐	Grooming tools
☐	Dog food	☐	Chew toys
☐	Leash	☐	Toys
☐	Collar	☐	ID tag
☐	Crate		

There are likely to be a few other items that you're dying to pick up before bringing your dog home. Use the following blanks to note any additional items you'll be shopping for.

☐ _____

☐ _____

☐ _____

☐ _____

☐ _____

☐ _____

☐ _____

☐ _____

☐ _____

☐ _____

☐ _____

☐ _____

Pet Sitter's Guide

We can be reached at (___)_____-_____ Cellphone (___)_____-_____

_____

We will return on _____ (date) at _____ (approximate time)

Dog's Name _____

Breed, Age, and Sex _____

Important Names and Numbers

Vet's Name _____ Phone (___)_____- _____

Address _____

Emergency Vet's Name _____ Phone (___)_____- _____

Address _____

Poison Control _____ (or call vet first)

Other individual to contact in case of emergency _____

_____

Care Instructions

In the following three blanks let the sitter know what to feed, how much, and when; when the dog should go out; when to give treats; and when to exercise the dog.

Morning _____

_____

Afternoon _____

_____

Evening _____

_____

Medications needed (dosage and schedule) _____

_____

Any special medical conditions _____

_____

Grooming instructions _____

_____

My dog's favorite playtime activities, quirks, and other tips_____

_____

_____

Part I
The World of the Dachshund

The Dachshund

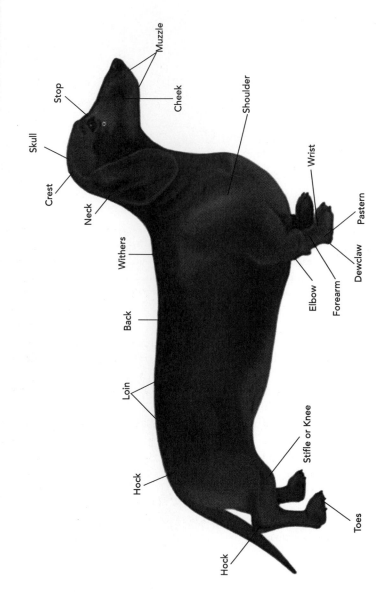

Muzzle

Cheek

Stop

Skull

Crest

Neck

Shoulder

Wrist

Pastern

Dewclaw

Forearm

Elbow

Withers

Back

Loin

Hock

Stifle or Knee

Toes

Hock

Chapter 1

What Is a Dachshund?

Throughout the world there are more than 300 breeds of dogs, but few are more distinctive or more easily recognized than the Dachshund. Anyone who has once seen a Dachshund is unlikely to confuse him with any other breed. In addition to the Dachshund's unusual physical appearance, his character, temperament, and behavior are as unique as the shape of his body.

The Dachshund has been in the top ten most popular breeds in American Kennel Club (AKC) registration for many years and is a popular breed in many countries the world over. What is it that makes the Dachshund a favorite choice of so many, and why has his popularity endured? A dozen Dachshund owners would probably give a dozen different answers to these questions. And therein lies the Dachshund's appeal. In comparison to most other breeds, this is one of the most diverse, versatile, and adaptable.

What are the special characteristics of the Dachshund that make him a Dachshund? The official breed standard of the Dachshund spells these out in great detail. The first breed standard for the Dachshund was written in Germany in 1879 and was adopted, with certain modifications, by the Dachshund Club of America (DCA), which came into being in 1895. The first official standard written by the DCA was written and approved by the American Kennel Club in July of 1935. Since the first Dachshund standard was adopted by the DCA, it has undergone two revisions.

What Is a Breed Standard?

A breed standard is a detailed description of the perfect dog of that breed. Breeders use the standard as a guide in their breeding programs, and judges use it to evaluate the dogs in conformation shows. The standard is written by the national breed club, using guidelines established by the registry that recognizes the breed (such as the AKC or UKC).

The first section of the breed standard describes the dog's general appearance and size as an adult. Next is a detailed description of the head and neck, then the back and body, and the front and rear legs. The standard then describes the ideal coat and how the dog should be presented in the show ring. It also lists all acceptable colors, patterns, and markings. Then there's a section on how the dog moves, called *gait*. Finally, there's a general description of the dog's temperament.

Each section also lists characteristics that are considered to be faults or disqualifications in the conformation ring. Superficial faults in appearance are often what distinguish a pet-quality dog from a show or competition-quality dog. However, some faults affect the way a dog moves or his overall health. And faults in temperament are serious business.

You can read all the AKC breed standards at www.akc.org.

Built for Hunting

Before looking at the details of the breed standard, let's look at what the Dachshund was bred to do. First and foremost, the Dachshund is a hunting dog. The breed was originally developed to hunt badger, a formidable adversary. His unique body type was designed specifically to hunt badgers in their underground burrows, but his powerful hunting instincts make him an excellent trailing dog as well. Courage and determination are essential in the dogs performing this task.

The Dachshund should always exhibit the structure and temperament traits that are necessary for him to perform effectively below and above ground, and

The Dachshund was bred to hunt.

the modern descendant of the old badger hunter still does. The Dachshund of today has lost none of the determination, fire, and pluck of his ancestors. To put it bluntly, in spite of his relatively small size, the Dachshund is not a wimp.

The Dachshund standard begins with a section called General Appearance, and the first sentence in that section is, "Low to ground, long in body and short of leg with robust muscular development, the skin is elastic and pliable without excessive wrinkling." Although the body of the Dachshund is longer than the body of most breeds and is a key physical characteristic that gives the Dachshund his distinctive appearance, it must present a look of sturdiness and strength. If the body is too long and/or too slender, the impression is that of weakness and ineffectiveness.

To work effectively underground, the standard says the Dachshund must have "well-sprung ribs ample enough and oval enough to allow complete development of heart and lungs, with the keel merging gradually into the line of the abdomen and extending well beyond the front legs." In other words, the dog must have the capacity to breathe underground and the muscular agility that enables him to maneuver when he pursues his quarry into an underground burrow (called "going to ground"). He needs to be low enough to slide into a burrow and yet have enough leg under him to prevent injury to himself. His hindquarters must be strong enough to propel him forward and to keep his keel (the rounded part of the lower chest) and powerful forechest from scraping the ground. It is the balance of his forequarters and hindquarters working together, along with the elasticity of his muscles, that enables this hound to move with ease through a maze of underground tunnels.

He must be muscular, with no skin loose enough to enable his prey to grab hold, which is why the standard states that there should be no wrinkles or dewlap (loose, hanging skin on the chin, throat, and neck). The skin of the Dachshund is comparable to a good piece of knit clothing: It should fit close to the body and yet stretch to allow him to move and bend as necessary.

In the hunting Dachshund we need stamina over speed. Short-legged hounds hunt with endurance. Therefore, the structure of the forequarters and the hindquarters of this hunting hound must be strong, powerful, and correct. If these aspects of the Dachshund are not correct, it hampers his performance and his stamina, and thus may cause him injury when he is working.

Many people poke fun at this short-legged, long little dog. However, it is important to remember that while most Dachshund owners may never use their dog to hunt, he was bred to hunt! He is powerful, muscular, and athletic. In the field, he must "give tongue." This means that there are times when he is working in the field that he must bark. It also means he will bark at home.

The Dachshund follows his prey by scent, not sight, and when he hunts he is single-minded. The Dachshund's nose, with the help of his long ears (which funnel scent to his nose), picks up the scent and he is off on his mission to track

Dachshunds hunt by scent, and bark when they find their prey.

his prey, dig to the quarry, corner it, and bark to alert the above-ground hunter to exactly where in the myriad of underground dens the animals are. If he did not "give tongue" as he worked, the hunters would be hard pressed to follow, as the Dachshund does not travel in a straight line when tracking, and once he has gone to ground locating him would indeed be a challenge if not for the melodious alert of a dog who has cornered his prey. Then the hunter can either dig to the Dachshund or assist the dog in retreating from underground if he does not emerge on his own with his prey.

The Dachshund must have agility, freedom of movement, and endurance to do the work for which the breed was developed. When the Dachshund moves, the standard says his gait should be "fluid and smooth." His forelegs should "reach well forward without much lift." Simply put, he should not paddle the air or prance. Such movements are wasted energy for a dog bred for stamina.

Viewed from the front, the legs do not move in exact parallel planes but incline slightly inward. This has to happen due to the shortness of the legs and the width of the chest. When the moving dog is viewed from the rear, the standard says "the thrust of correct movement is seen when the pads [of the hind feet] are clearly exposed." To keep the topline (the dog's outline from just behind the top of the shoulders to the tail) level in motion, each vertebrae must be supported by ribs, tendons, pelvis, and muscles. This means, simply, that the length of ribs and topline must balance one another.

The Dachshund temperament is what makes him such a delightful and versatile breed. The standard states, "The Dachshund is clever, lively, and courageous to the point of rashness, persevering in above and below ground work, with all the senses well-developed. Any display of shyness is a serious fault." A Dachshund who is shy or fearful could not carry out the work he was bred to do. If he doesn't possess the temperament traits specified in the standard, all the other desirable structural qualities lose their significance.

What is the typical overall demeanor of this sturdy hound? The standard says he should be bold and confident in the carriage of his head and possess an "intelligent, alert facial expression." How does this translate to your Dachshund? You will know what it means when you see those expressive eyes that grab you with their alert "I love the world" attitude and a head carriage that says, "The world is a challenge and I can tackle anything. Want to see?"

That Elegant Head

Part of what gives the Dachshund his wonderful look is his clean, elegant head, set on a neck the standard describes as "long, muscular, clean-cut . . . slightly arched in the nape, flowing gracefully into the shoulders."

The head should be elegant and tapering, with a finely formed, slightly arched muzzle.

The eyes are dark, of medium size, and almond-shaped, with what the standard calls "an energetic, pleasant expression." The bridge bones over the eyes should be strongly prominent. The ears are set near the top of the head, not too far forward, are of moderate length, and rounded. When the dog is animated, the ears should come forward to frame his face.

The head should taper uniformly to the tip of the nose. The skull slopes gradually into the finely-formed, slightly arched muzzle.

Sizes

One aspect of the Dachshund's diversity is that he comes in two sizes—Standard and Miniature. While there is no absolute weight limit for the Standard, the Dachshund Club of America suggests that he range from sixteen to thirty-two pounds. The Miniature has specific weight guidelines: At 12 months of age he must be eleven pounds or under, and should remain so if he is to compete in dog shows.

Other than weight, there is no difference mentioned in the standard between the two sizes. Since the Dachshund is a dog of substance and stamina, both sizes should possess "robust muscular development." The bone and substance of the Miniature should be appropriate for his size. The breed standard by which he is judged is the same as that for the Standard Dachshund.

Coat Types

Another aspect of Dachshund diversity is that the breed comes in three coat varieties—smooth (shorthaired), longhaired, and wirehaired. The smooth coat is the short, shiny, flat coat that most people associate with Dachshunds, and is certainly the most common. In fact, many people are not aware that Dachshunds come any other way.

The longhair has the same body configuration as the smooth, but has a coat of medium length that lies close to the body, with longer hair on the ears, the back of the legs, the underside of the tail and body, and the front of the chest. This longer hair is called feathering. The overall appearance is much like that of an Irish Setter. This difference in the coat gives the longhair a softer, gentler appearance.

Like the longhair, the wirehair Dachshund has a body type comparable to that of the smooth, but it is covered with a coarse, wiry coat like that of a terrier, complete with a similar beard and bushy eyebrows. This tough coat gives the wirehair a sturdy, rugged look that seems to impart the message that this Dachshund is not afraid of anything.

Underneath all three coats, there is still a Dachshund. However, there are some small differences in each variety's outlook and demeanor, as well as the amount of care required to maintain each coat. (Care of each coat type will be addressed in chapter 7.)

In general, smooths can be independent little critters who often have a mind of their own to the point of, at times, being rather stubborn. While this trait can really try one's patience sometimes, in a way it adds to their charm. After all, a perpetual "yes man" can become rather boring. Since, historically, the smooth was most likely the original variety, it would seem to follow that smooths embody more of typical Dachshund traits. This unpredictable behavior does offer a challenge, though.

The smooth, wirehaired, and longhaired varieties each have their own personalities.

The longhair's demeanor seems to reflect his softer, gentler overall appearance. Longhairs seem to be the somewhat more laidback variety. But don't let this kinder, gentler manner fool you. They are often the most avid hunters and are quite effective in field work.

The wirehair is probably the least known of the three varieties. The rough, wiry, double coat definitely imparts the look of a terrier. Just as the longhair's appearance seems to characterize his deportment, the wirehair displays many traits usually attributed to terriers. Wirehairs can be characterized as brash, fiery, and bold. They seem to enjoy creating a conflict. Don't be put off by this bold, impertinent facade. Beneath all the bluster, there still lies a Dachshund with all his endearing charms.

Colors and Patterns

If you are beginning to think Dachshunds are really a pretty diverse breed, there's more. Not only do Dachshunds come in different sizes and coat types, they also come in many coat colors and can have coat patterns. Since there is such a profusion of coat colors and patterns, this is an area that can be confusing and even, at times, controversial.

Colors

The colors most common in Dachshunds are red and a combination of black and tan. Surprisingly, I have found many people who are not aware that Dachshunds can be black and tan.

The term "red" covers a wide variety of hues, ranging from a very light shade, more like a reddish blonde, to a deep, russet red. Many reds have black hairs interspersed among the red. Another single color is cream—an apt description for a very light color. Cream is not a common color, though, and thus is not one many people are aware of or have ever seen.

Black and tans are referred to as two-colored Dachshunds. A black and tan is a dog who is basically all black with tan markings on various parts of his body, most notably on the head, chest, and paws. These tan points, as they are often called, have the same range of shading as the reds. Other two-colored Dachshunds include chocolate, gray (which is usually referred to as "blue") and fawn (which is often called Isabella). All of these colors have the same distinguishing tan markings as the black and tans.

A color called wild boar mixes light hairs with black ones and many shades in between throughout the dog's coat. This gives the dog a salt-and-pepper look. Wild boar is most commonly found in wirehairs.

This Miniature shows the controversial piebald coat.

Patterns

In addition to a variety of colors, Dachshund coats can also have patterns. The dapple pattern is characterized by lighter areas and markings over the dog's body that contrast with a darker base color. The double dapple pattern is one in which varying amounts of white occur over the body in addition to the dappling spots. Brindle is distinguished by dark stripes all over the dog's body.

Relatively recently, a pattern called piebald (which is not mentioned in the Dachshund breed standard), has appeared on the scene. A piebald dog has large areas of white on his body, which otherwise can be any one of the aforementioned colors. At present, there is ongoing controversy surrounding this pattern and its acceptability in the show ring. A final decision on the matter has not yet been made.

Chapter 2

The Dachshund's History

The early history of the Dachshund is often woven through with legends, stories, and artifacts that have come down to us through the ages. The origin of this amazing little dog has been a subject of much speculation. As with many writers of breed histories, some writers of Dachshund history have suggested that the Dachshund had its beginnings in the ancient past. Many writers refer to carvings of small, short-legged, long-bodied, doglike animals that appeared on monuments in ancient Egypt, as well as to other carvings or statues of animals with similar characteristics that were found in ancient ruins in Mexico, China, and Greece. When all is said and done, these theories of ancient beginnings remain mostly conjecture.

The Dachshund's Roots

It is probable that short-legged dogs used for hunting coexisted in France, Germany, and other western European countries centuries ago, and that these dogs evolved in their native lands along separate lines. It is relatively certain, based on historical writings and woodcuts, that small Dachshund-like dogs called bassets were used for hunting in the sixteenth century. The term "basset" is the French word for "low," and was used to describe dogs who were low in stature with long, rather slender bodies, and legs that were somewhat turned in with feet that were inclined to turn outward.

Although there is no known concrete evidence of the breed crossings that went into the development of the breed that became known as the Dachshund, the low stature, the outturned feet that were characteristic of early specimens, and the keen nose would seem to suggest a common ancestry with the Basset Hound. The fact that no other hound goes to ground seems to imply that somewhere along the line, the Dachshund probably received an infusion of terrier blood.

Many kinds of dogs originally filled the function of badger hunters.

It appears that as early as the Middle Ages, there were many dogs who filled the function of hunting badgers without necessarily meeting the Dachshund's description. The name Dachshund, which means "badger dog" in German, seems to have been first used near the end of the seventeenth century. It was at this time that the term "badger dog" definitely designated both the smooth and longhaired Dachshunds as they are known today.

Whatever theories one holds concerning the original home of the ancestral stock from which the breed evolved, the Dachshund as we know her today was developed and refined by German foresters into what they needed—a fearless hunter with intelligence who could work above and below ground over various terrains, and who was obstinate and rash enough to hold her prey at bay (which ranged from rabbit and fox to badger and wild boar) until the hunter could finish the deed. This is where the Dachshund's loud, threatening bark came in handy. A pack of Dachshunds giving tongue can be a formidable, frightening foe.

Developing the Modern Dachshund

A stud book is a record of the parentage of dogs of a particular breed. The name of each individual dog is recorded, along with the names of the dog's parents. There were fifty-four Dachshunds registered in the German all-breed stud book in 1840. By 1879 the first breed standard for the Dachshund was developed. It was quite a detailed standard, and few changes have been made in the standard since that time.

The Germans often use the word "teckel" when referring to Dachshunds. Thus it is not surprising that the first Dachshund breed club, established in 1888, was called the Berlin Teckelclub. In 1890, the first stud book devoted solely to Dachshunds was published and there were 394 Dachshunds listed in it.

The recorded development of the Dachshund in Britain occurred almost simultaneously with the advent of formal record-keeping in Germany. The first Dachshunds came to Britain in 1840. Show records indicate they first appeared in shows in 1860 and were exhibited as German Badger Hounds. They were entered in the British stud book in 1874 as Dachshunds, but this term was followed by German Badger Dog in parentheses. The British Dachshund Club was formed in 1881—earlier than the Berlin Teckelclub.

Not only was the Dachshund a favorite among hunters, she was also popular with members of the European aristocracy, including many of the royal houses of Britain. In her diary, dated April 23, 1833, Britain's Queen Victoria referred to her Dachshund, whom she called Dash. Historical accounts show that her consort, Prince Albert, gave her the dog. A portrait painted in 1839 shows Queen Victoria with a Dachshund. While the queen kept her Dachshunds as lovable and devoted companions, it is said that Prince Albert used Dachshunds to hunt in Windsor Forest.

The Dachshund we know today was developed to be a fearless, intelligent hunter who could work above and below ground.

What Is a Breed Club?

A national breed club is an organization established to support a specific breed, and is often characterized as the guardian of the breed. National breed clubs are responsible for maintaining the written standard for their breed. They also provide assistance and resources to breeders and owners of the breed, as well as to local breed clubs throughout the country.

The Dachshund Club of America (DCA) is the national breed club for Dachshunds. It has been a member club of the AKC since 1895 and, as such, is one of the oldest breed clubs in the AKC. It has more than 1,500 members worldwide and it is the parent club to about 50 local Dachshund clubs throughout the country.

Local breed clubs ore organized by individuals in various parts of the country who have an interest in a particular breed. They meet to share their interest in the breed, and, like the national club, they strive to promote the well-being of the breed. They conduct various educational programs, fun events, and formal events, which can include conformation dog shows, field trials, obedience trials, and any other event that is approved by the AKC. If you would like to belong to a local Dachshund club, you can see if there is one in your area by visiting the DCA website at www.dachshund-dca.org.

Never a country to miss a trend, the interest in Dachshunds in the United States occurred almost simultaneously with the breed's recognition and development in Europe and Great Britain. According to AKC records, Dachshunds were recognized as a breed in 1885 and eleven were entered in what is now Volume I of the AKC Stud Book. In 1895, the Dachshund Club of America became a member club of the AKC.

The history of the Dachshund in the United States is a checkered one when it comes to breeding and popularity. Early breeding programs appeared to emphasize dogs imported from Europe, particularly Germany. These early Dachshund breeders knew little about the backgrounds of the dogs they acquired and had scant knowledge of successful breeding practices. Many early owners of Dachshunds, particularly on the East Coast, were strongly influenced by the early British breeders from whom they obtained their stock. However, over the years serious breeders developed sound breeding plans in the United States and many fine Dachshund bloodlines were established.

During the late 1800s and early 1900s, the Dachshund rapidly gained in popularity. By 1914, Dachshunds were among the top ten breeds exhibited at the Westminster Kennel Club Show. However, with the start of World War I, the popularity of Dachshunds declined abruptly, because of the breed's association with Germany. During this time, German breeding activity and breeding stock became almost nonexistent. Fortunately for the breed, there were dedicated individuals under whose guidance Dachshund breeding was reestablished in the United States, and the Dachshund quickly regained her popularity.

What Is the AKC?

The American Kennel Club (AKC) is the oldest and largest pure-bred dog registry in the United States. Its main function is to record the pedigrees of dogs of the breeds it recognizes. While AKC registration papers are a guarantee that a dog is pure-bred, they are absolutely not a guarantee of the quality of the dog—as the AKC itself will tell you.

The AKC makes the rules for all the canine sporting events it sanctions and approves judges for those events. This not-for-profit organization is devoted to the advancement and welfare of purebred dogs and dogs in general. As such, it is involved in various public education programs and legislative efforts regarding dog ownership. More recently, the AKC has helped establish a foundation to study canine health issues and a program to register microchip numbers for companion animal owners. The AKC has no individual members—its members are all-breed clubs, national breed clubs, and clubs dedicated to various competitive events.

World War II again was disastrous for German and British breeders, but by then breeders in the United States were well established and the popularity of Dachshunds continued to grow. This popularity extends to the present day, as evidenced by the fact that the Dachshund is consistently among the top ten most popular breeds registered by the American Kennel Club.

History of the Smooth Variety

It is widely accepted that the smooth variety was the first Dachshund to be developed. These were the early small hunting dogs who were referred to near the end of the seventeenth century as "badger dogs." The smooth Dachshund is the most popular variety in the United States and is the one that most people think of when they picture a Dachshund.

In the late 1930s, Josef and Maria Mehrer established the von Marienlust Kennel in West Hempstead, New York. This was a defining moment in the development of the Dachshund in the twentieth century, particularly in smooths. Josef and Maria were knowledgeable about the breed, and Josef was an astute breeder who had the knack for knowing what sires and dams clicked to produce the best offspring. Many of the breeders of that time founded their kennels

Smooths were the first variety to be developed.

using von Marienlust stock. A large number of our present-day smooth Dachshunds can be traced back to von Marienlust bloodlines.

Longhair Dachshund History

The longhair variety existed before the Dachshund was recognized as a breed. There are two theories about how the longhair Dachshund came about. Some breed historians believe it was developed from the original smooth Dachshund by selective breeding. Smooth Dachshunds would occasionally produce puppies who had slightly longer hair than their parents. By selectively breeding these dogs, breeders eventually produced a dog that consistently produced long hair. Another theory is that smooth Dachshunds were bred to various types of spaniels and the longhair was developed in this way. In either case, the result was a beautiful dog with a coat similar to that of an Irish Setter and a temperament more like that of a spaniel.

Breed historians are not exactly sure how the longhair came about. It may have begun as a natural mutation, or smooths may have been crossbred with spaniels.

There were several kennels and individuals that were instrumental in the development of the longhair in the United States. One name that invariably emerges in any discussion of longhairs is Mary Howell and her Bayard Kennel, located in Fairfax, Virginia. Through a well-thought-out breeding program, Howell produced longhairs who had a strong consistency of type and structure. The Bayard longhairs had beautiful heads, correct fronts, and long ribbing—all desirable qualities in a good Dachshund.

These essential traits were passed on to succeeding generations and Bayard Dachshunds were the foundation of many longhair kennels.

Wirehair Dachshund History

The wirehair Dachshund is a relatively recent development when compared to the smooths and longhairs. The wirehair's tough coat was developed to protect her as she trailed game through the thickets and dense undergrowth of the forests.

Because the wirehairs were bred almost solely by foresters for hunting purposes, pedigrees on these dogs were not kept until relatively recently, which makes it difficult to trace exactly when this variety emerged. In the early 1800s, a wirehair Dachshund was described as taller on leg than the smooth, with forelegs that curved but were less bent than in the smooth.

Breed historians theorize that the wire coat was produced by crosses with a rough-coated German Pinscher and the Dandie Dinmont Terrier—a terrier with short legs and a long body. The coat of both these breeds is wiry, short, thick, and rough, and they look very smart with their short beards and bushy eyebrows. Like their smooth cousins, wirehairs tend to be mischievous.

The wire coat is a relatively recent development, intended to protect a dog who hunts through dense undergrowth.

Two names almost automatically surface when thinking about dogs who had a strong influence on the present-day wirehairs: Ch. Vantebe's Draht Timothy, from New York, and Ch. Pondwick's Hobgoblin, who was imported from Britain. Both of these dogs made significant contributions to establishing a more consistent and desirable wire type. Combining the bloodlines from both of them proved to be quite successful in producing excellent wirehaired Dachshunds, and was instrumental in establishing the wire type that is seen today.

The Miniature Emerges

Miniature Dachshunds were developed in Germany by German hunters who wanted a smaller, lighter dog to hunt rabbits. They accomplished this by selectively breeding small Standards, and then breeding the smallest offspring from these litters until these smaller dogs emerged with more frequency and consistency. However, since the emphasis was on reducing size, often the dogs used in these breeding programs were bred solely because of their small size. Faults they may have had were ignored. As a result, most of the early Miniatures were not quality dogs.

Miniatures were developed in Germany by hunters who wanted a smaller dog to trail rabbits.

It is difficult to name any one breeder who developed the Miniature as we know her today. Nor are there one or two individual dogs who can be credited with establishing our present-day Miniatures. There were numerous dedicated Miniature breeders in all parts of the country who worked tirelessly to produce quality Miniature Dachshunds.

Miniatures were imported to the United States around 1930. During the early years of Miniature breeding in the United States, there were not many of these small dogs. Most were either imports or their immediate descendants. This made it difficult to develop sound breeding plans. Plans that were developed were even harder to carry out. All Miniature stock had comparatively recent ancestors of Standard size or ancestors in which faults linked with too rapid size reduction were concentrated.

> **Famous Dachshund Owners**
>
> Noël Coward
> Errol Flynn
> Clark Gable
> Paulette Goddard
> William Randolph Hearst
> Carole Lombard
> Pablo Picasso
> Liz Smith
> Queen Victoria
> Andy Warhol
> John Wayne
> E. B. White

Whenever fairly close linebreeding was attempted to expedite a program, two outcomes were likely to occur: First, improved quality usually brought with it increased size. Second, if the breeding produced small dogs, they usually had the same faults that were seen in the Miniatures found in Germany—fiddle fronts (forearms out, elbows in, feet out), light frames, pop eyes, pointy muzzles, apple-domed heads, and bad ears.

By the end of the 1940s, Miniatures had become popular with the public as pets. They were cute and their small size appealed to many. They were perfect dogs for small apartments and urban living. There were several breeders who devoted their efforts to breeding better Miniatures. By the late 1950s, Mrs. William Burr Hill, Lydia Beard, Mrs. Dwight Garner, Muriel Glenz, Mrs. O'Doud, Charlie Mays, and Mr. and Mrs. James Ruffel were among those who were striving to breed better Miniatures.

It is not possible to give enough praise to the Miniature breeders who worked so long and so diligently to develop the present-day Miniature. It took many decades of dedication. The lovely Miniatures we see today are the fruits of their labor.

Chapter 3

Why Choose a Dachshund?

Although there are many other breeds I admire, the Dachshund is the dog for me. Dachshunds have enriched my life by adding the kind of joy, delight, devotion, and companionship that only they can bring. Dachshunds can try your patience one minute and make you giggle with delight the next. There is nothing to compare to a Dachshund's expression when he looks lovingly at you with those wonderful, affectionate eyes, or to the joy that is reflected in his whole demeanor as he excitedly and eagerly greets you when you return after being away for even a short time.

He is such an amiable dog, and he loves to go places and do things with you. And you can do so many things with him. His small size makes it easy for him to be comfortable in almost any setting. It also makes him a suitable traveling companion. With his intelligence, cleverness, curiosity, and hunting instincts, he is able to learn to do many things and can successfully participate in many activities. He can hunt, track, and follow obedience commands. He will be a faithful companion, will protect your home, and will make you laugh. And on top of all that, you have three choices of coat, two size options, and many colors and patterns. What more could you ask?

The Dachshund was bred to hunt badgers—formidable foes. Courage and determination were essential in the dogs performing this task. These qualities are still strongly characteristic of the modern descendant of the old badger hunter. Dachshunds are very brave, rather stubborn, and have a tendency to be somewhat independent.

Although he still possesses those qualities that made him so successful in the field, the modern Dachshund is, for the most part, a house dog—a role for which he is well-suited. His size enables him to fit comfortably in a house or an apartment. And his temperament enables him to fit easily into your family and your heart. This is a vivacious little dog who radiates an endearing charm and an overwhelming, authentic joy of living. He is clever, clean, adaptable, versatile, good-tempered, loyal, inquisitive, fun-loving, playful, alert, intelligent, and endowed with a dignity not often found in dogs of his dimensions. All of these virtues, combined with his intensely affectionate nature, make the Dachshund an ideal companion.

A Hunting Hound

Remembering that a Dachshund is a scent hound will save you a lot of aggravation. His nose is extraordinary! Dachshunds can smell candy wrappers in a wastepaper basket, a speck of food under a cabinet, a well-aged crumb behind the refrigerator. If your dog tells you something is lurking out of your sight, believe him!

This breed hunts—anything. Scents appeal to him. Following them is what he was bred to do. Because of this, he should *never* be off leash unless he is in a secure, confined area. Once he gets the scent of an animal, he is single-minded and will be off. Even if he has been trained to respond to commands, if he picks up a scent, he'll go after it!

Your little hound will delight, surprise, and exasperate you. (This pup has a dapple pattern.)

If you are out walking with him, *always* have him on a leash. I know that this may cramp his style, because your Dachshund will love to explore anything he finds interesting along the way and his leash may not be long enough to allow him this pleasure. But be steadfast in your resolve to keep him safe from harm.

Dachshunds are strong-willed and tend to do what they please. But they still want to please you.

Because this breed is so curious, it is easy for him to get into almost anything. Dachshunds don't worry or wonder what something is or how it tastes—they investigate! They have strong jaws, strong teeth, and a relentless determination once they have decided to get something that they want. They have been known to eat right through a linoleum floor because someone spilled gravy on it, or to eat the pocket out of an expensive jacket to get to a few pieces of dog treats. Believe me, it is much easier to keep things away from a Dachshund than to keep him away from things. Remember that. It will save you a lot of trouble and a lot of money.

The Dachshund is also persistent. He will jump on the furniture no matter how many times you tell him "no!"—unless you remain firm and do not give in. Being mischievous, he will test you. Being sly, he will do it if he thinks you're not around. Being intelligent, he will get down when he hears you coming or if you are forceful in your command to get off the sofa. To be honest, it is easier to cover the chair or the sofa, or to keep him out of any room you don't want him to claim as his own. Yet, as active as the Dachshund is, he is a lap dog, a sleep-next-to-you-in-the-chair dog, a curl-up-at-your-feet-in-the-bed dog.

Quick, Playful, Hungry!

Despite the jokes made about his shape, the Dachshund is quick and agile. Chasing and running after him is a no-win situation for you. Standing still is the best thing to do, because if you feign interest in something and seem to be ignoring him, his curiosity will eventually win out and he'll give up the keep-away game and come to investigate. Hopefully!

This little dog loves toys and balls and paper-towel tubes and will amuse himself for hours if his people won't play with him. Many Dachshunds will retrieve but will not necessarily surrender their toy. It is not good to engage in a tug of war with your dog at any time, but especially when he is a puppy. This kind of play can encourage aggressive and/or defiant behavior. Because his teeth and jaws are so strong, you will not win this battle, and he will take your inability to get whatever the two of you are tugging on as a sign of weakness on your part—which can lead to him becoming defiant or aggressive in other situations.

Expect your Dachshund to pester you for food if you don't train him not to. He is a beggar, and more often than not he will eat anything. He will steal food, given the chance, and be a pest if allowed. Ban him from the kitchen and dining room until you have trained him to stay away from the counters and table. Although it is very difficult to resist those pleading eyes with that "I'm really starving" look, the best strategy is to *never* give him any food while you are eating. Don't let him do once what you don't want him to do forever!

Of course, this is very difficult to do—especially when he is a puppy. He is just *too cute* and it is hard to resist his pleas. But take my word for it: If you succumb to his irresistible charms, he will be a constant pest and then it will be difficult to get him to stop his annoying begging. This isn't to say that he won't sit and stare at you when you have food or follow you into the kitchen if he thinks he might have a chance to persuade you to give him a morsel of something, but he will not jump up, bark, or do other things to try to get you to give him just one crumb.

Dachshunds love to eat and they will eat almost anything. This is good, you say. Who wants to have a finicky eater?

Dachshunds do love their toys. It's best not to play tug of war with your puppy.

However, many Dachshunds seem to have no sense of how much food they can reasonably consume. As long as there is food around, they will eat it.

Therefore it is always wise to keep all—and I mean *all*—food out of their reach. Fortunately, because the Dachshund is low to ground and thus cannot reach too high, food put on countertops and dinner tables is usually safe. I say "usually" because, if you remember, Dachshunds are clever and intelligent. If there is a way to get to the food, they will find it.

I remember a night in our house when someone forgot to push a chair under the table after we finished eating dinner. Dessert, which was to be eaten later, was left in the center of the table. This particular dessert was an Easter cake shaped like a lamb, complete with coconut coating and a tiny bell on a ribbon tied around the lamb's neck. Everyone left the house for awhile to visit a friend. Upon returning, we found that the entire cake had disappeared. Not even a crumb could be found. Fortunately, the little bell and ribbon were on the kitchen floor. Can you believe a Dachshund could jump up on a chair, then get on the table, take the cake down by the same route and carry it to the kitchen, where it was totally consumed? It happened!

Dachshunds are definitely chow hounds. These Minis would jump their height for that morsel, if they could.

Dachshunds and Families

The Dachshund is not normally a one-person dog, although he may prefer some family members over others. A well-bred Dachshund's temperament is cordial and outgoing. He is mildly wary of strangers and makes an excellent watchdog.

Properly introduced to children, he accepts them willingly and makes an ideal companion for them. Common sense is the secret here. Most experts believe it is unwise to match children under the age of 6 with a young puppy. In my experience, 7 might be a better age unless the 6-year-old is mature for her age and well-behaved. Younger children may treat the puppy as a doll and do things such as putting the dog in a wagon and then pushing it over, or trying to brush his hair too roughly and hurting the puppy. Small children like to pick things up and carry them around, too. If they do this with a puppy, they may hold him too tightly or drop him if he tries to get out of their grasp.

With this kind of treatment, it doesn't take a young dog very long to learn that it is best to avoid small children by running away or hiding, which makes things even worse. When this happens, a small child may try to pull the puppy out by his ears, paws, or tail. Is it any wonder that such a puppy will then growl or snap at a child? If a Dachshund does not seem to be very good with children, he probably had some unhappy and unpleasant experiences with them at an early age.

Older children should be taught the proper and considerate ways to handle and interact with a dog. Dachshunds and children can be great companions. If they are introduced to each other under the right conditions and at the right age and time, they will be able to share a lifetime of love, trust, and fun.

It will be up to you to make sure guests who are welcomed to your home are introduced to your Dachshund.

> ### CAUTION
>
> **Watch Out for Cars!**
>
> Dachshunds enjoy riding in cars but they appear to have no fear or sense of the danger cars present on the street, and will walk right in front of them. In addition to not having a clue about cars, the fact that Dachshunds are so low to the ground makes it very difficult for anyone driving a car to see them. I cannot stress strongly enough that you should never—and I mean *never*—allow your Dachshund to be off a short leash anywhere there is a possibility of coming in contact with cars.

He is an alert watchdog and needs to be told it is all right for this person to come into his domain. A Dachshund who has been properly socialized will readily accept anyone you accept.

Well-bred Dachshunds are happy-go-lucky and want to get into anyone's lap. Some people may not appreciate that! While not happy about this, your Dachshund should respect their feelings even if he doesn't understand them. Be careful that your dog does not slip out the door while you are greeting guests, as he might take off if there is something outside that catches his fancy.

The Dachshund loves to see what is going on around him. He is very rarely a side-liner, a bystander, or a wallflower. His front lawn, his street, next door, and down the block are part of his territory, and he cares about what happens there. He watches and he listens and he barks! Constant barking can become a problem. With proper training, this annoying behavior can be brought under control. But be assured that no one will be able to sneak up on you without you knowing about it.

Dachshunds are people-oriented dogs and will be mildly wary of strangers.

The Dachshund is a pack dog and loves to be with others of his own kind. Having more than one Dachshund in your home can be quite pleasurable for you and for him. At present, I live with two Dachshunds, Libby and Johann. I had Libby first. There were occasions when Libby and I spent some time with a friend who had many Dachshunds, and I saw how much Libby loved to play and interact with the other dogs. When we returned home after these visits, she would just lie around and appeared to be brooding as if she were thinking about the good times she had with her friends. So I decided she needed to have a friend of her own, and that is how Johann became part of our household. The two of them are best friends. It's a joy to watch them play or see them sleeping curled up next to each other on the sofa.

If you decide to have two Dachshunds, it is wise to have a male and a female. Two Dachshunds of the same sex can have dominance problems, which can lead to down and out fights, which you *absolutely* do not want to have. Remember, Dachshunds were bred to hunt badgers. They can do a lot of significant damage to one another if they get into a serious fight. And once they have fought, it is likely they will do it again.

A Dachshund can be tolerant of cats if they are introduced properly or if he grows up with them in the family. Other people's cats are fair game, though! Hamsters and rabbits are natural prey to him and should *never* be on the same level, loose or caged, with this hound.

As adorable as they are, it's easy to forget that Dachshunds are hunting hounds.

A Faithful Companion

A Dachshund just loves to be with people; it's as simple as that. He'll stay where you are and go where you go. He always wants to be with you. If you don't want a dog who follows you everywhere and is almost always underfoot, the Dachshund is probably not for you. Their love and devotion to you can, at times, be almost too much—but not for long. They will always manage to win your love.

Since you are the center of their world, Dachshunds are always trying to get your attention. They will use every means possible to accomplish this. At first, they will try routines that have worked for them in the past. When these fail, they will invent new ones. This is when they call upon their sense of humor, as well as their cleverness, to impress you. As you observe your dog's antics, it won't be long before you can't help but laugh at his performance and give in to whatever it was he wanted you to do.

These dogs know what they like and what they want, but that doesn't mean they won't try their best to please you.

A Dachshund's favorite place to sleep is in your bed, preferably with you in it. If this isn't your preference, you will have a battle of wills. Guess who usually wins the war? This doesn't mean every Dachshund ends up sleeping on someone's bed. Even though almost every Dachshund aspires to this goal, if you are firm about your position, eventually his deep desire to please you will prevail and he will reluctantly accept your decision and sleep in his dog bed.

Having been involved with this breed for more than forty-five years, I can assure you there's no dog like a Dachshund. No companion as comical, as loving, or as adaptable. His goal in life is to love you, to protect you, and to be your very best friend.

Once you are owned by a Dachshund, you will never come into a room or a house you've left, even if it was only to take out the garbage or bring in the newspaper, without this delightful little hound greeting you with his tail beating the floor, so happy you've returned to his world.

Chapter 4

Choosing Your Dachshund

If you have decided the Dachshund is the breed for you, there are many things you should think about before you actually get a puppy or adult dog. You may have given a lot of thought to the coat variety, size, and color you think you would like. You may have decided whether you prefer a male or a female. As you begin your search for the dog who is right for you, these initial choices may change, so keep an open mind.

Let me offer this advice: Take your time in acquiring your Dachshund. This is not something that should be done in haste. It is not wise to rush out and buy the first cute puppy who catches your eye. *All* puppies are cute! Whether you want a dog to show in conformation competition, to compete with in performance events, or to be simply a family dog, the more time and effort you invest in choosing your Dachshund, the more likely you are to be happy with your choice.

Deciding on the Basics

As you learned in chapter 1, the Dachshund offers a lot of choices in coat type, color, and size. The choice you make depends on personal preference and your particular circumstances. Just remember that no matter what your final choice, you will still have a Dachshund who possesses the traits, characteristics, and personality of this wonderful breed.

The slight differences in temperament in each coat variety have been discussed. But just to review: The smooths are generally independent critters, and their coat requires the least amount of care; longhairs are less strong willed and more laid back, but their coat requires more grooming; and wirehairs have traits that are similar to terriers in that they can be brash and somewhat feisty, and their coat requires more grooming than the smooths.

As for size, Standard Dachshunds usually weigh between sixteen and thirty-two pounds. At maturity males are usually larger than females, but this is not always the case. Although the Standard Dachshund is not a large dog, she is a compact, muscular dog, which makes her heavy and *strong* for her size, especially if her weight is near the top of the weight range. Because of her spirited and rambunctious nature, she does require a fair amount of indoor space.

The official definition of a Miniature Dachshund is that she may not weigh more than eleven pounds at 1 year of age. However, this criterion is only for competition in the show ring. There are many Miniature Dachshunds who weigh more than eleven pounds, and they can weigh up to sixteen pounds. They cannot be shown as Miniatures in conformation competition, but they can compete in other AKC events. These are still small dogs when compared to a Standard. Because of their size, they are considerably easier to lift and certainly easier to manage than Standards. This makes them a good choice for small or elderly dog owners. Miniatures are also ideal for those who have a very small living area. They require much less space to be comfortable than do the Standards.

Start by deciding what coat type and size you want. These are all Minis.

Coat colors were discussed in detail in chapter 1. The most common color is solid red; the second most common is black and tan. Again, your choice depends on personal preference.

Gathering Information

There is an impressive array of resources available that can provide you with a wealth of information about Dachshunds. Many of these are listed in the appendix and in the online bonus elements. Reading more about Dachshunds is important, but reading about something and actually seeing it are quite different. That's why I recommend that you also attend some dog shows in your area, if you possibly can.

If there are shows held within a reasonable driving distance, it is well worth your time and effort to go to at least one. This is especially important if you have not really decided which coat variety you would like to have. If you have never seen a longhair or a wirehair Dachshund, it's likely examples of each will be at the show. If you are really lucky, there may be a Dachshund specialty show within driving distance. Only Dachshunds are shown at a Dachshund specialty show, and this is a great opportunity to see many Dachshunds in all varieties, both sizes, and possibly some colors and patterns that are not commonly seen.

Dog shows are a good place to look at Dachshunds and meet breeders.

You can get information about where and when all-breed dog shows and specialty shows are being held in your area on the AKC web site (www.akc.org): Go to the "Events" section and follow the instructions. You will be able to look up dates and locations for dog shows all over the country.

In addition to seeing the dogs, attending an all-breed or a specialty show provides an opportunity to talk to Dachshund breeders and owners. They will be more than willing to talk to you about Dachshunds and try to answer any questions you may have. You may find you really hit it off with a particular breeder, and that's a good start toward finding the person you want to get your Dachshund from.

Finding a Good Dachshund Breeder

Where do you look for a Dachshund? With few exceptions, the answer is to contact a responsible breeder. Why is it so important to get your dog from a responsible breeder? Because responsible breeders always put the best interests of the breed and of individual dogs first. They place this far above any consideration of profit or personal ambition.

Responsible breeders do not produce a litter just to have some puppies to sell or just because a bitch happened to come into season. Their goal is to

Look for a breeder whose goal is to produce excellent Dachshunds who conform to the breed standard.

improve the quality of the dogs they breed by producing litters of healthy puppies whose physical attributes and temperament move the breed toward the ideal Dachshund described in the standard. Because of the personal investment of time and effort they put into planning a litter, serious breeders more than likely consider the puppies as their kids and want only what is best for them.

Why is all of this important? You're probably not looking for a show dog; most people are just looking for a pet, a loving companion to enrich their lives. So are all of these things really necessary?

For the most part, the responsible breeder's primary purpose for breeding is to produce excellent examples of the breed who can compete in dog shows. In addition to possessing desirable physical attributes, the dogs must also have good, stable temperaments to deal with the rigors of show competition. You may have no interest in showing your Dachshund, but you may be interested in participating in some of the other activities that are available to you and your Dachshund. To be successful in these areas, your dog must have good physical conformation and a sound temperament.

Putting dog shows and performance events aside, the most important reason you should want a dog who has a stable personality is so you can enjoy your life with her. Your Dachshund should be a delight to have around. A shy, cowering dog, one with a nasty disposition, or maybe a fear biter is not my idea of a dog who brings joy into your life.

If you want a healthy, sound Dachshund with a good temperament, who is a fabulous pet and a good example of the breed, the best place to get such a dog is from a responsible breeder.

As you begin your search for your puppy, always keep one thought in mind: You are looking for a permanent member of your household. Be patient and use common sense and you will find a good breeder. The effort will be well worth it. Not only will you find the dog you have been hoping for, but you will also find someone who will provide you with support and is committed to making your relationship with your dog a rewarding one.

Finding a Breeder Through Referrals

If you are unable to attend a dog show, there are other ways to find a responsible breeder. If you have a relative, a friend, or a neighbor who has a Dachshund you like, ask who bred their dog. Word of mouth can be an excellent way to find a responsible breeder, especially since the better breeders usually do little advertising. Because of their good reputation, many of their puppies are often spoken for before they are born (or soon after), so they have no need to advertise widely. If they have no puppies or adult dogs available when you contact them, it is quite likely they know other responsible breeders to whom you can be referred.

If you are unable to get a personal referral, visit the Dachshund Club of America web site (www.dachshund-dca.org) and click on "Breeder Referrals." There, Dachshund breed clubs will be listed by state, along with contact information for the person in charge of breeder referrals for each club. This person can provide you with names and phone numbers of breeders in your area. The American Kennel Club also sponsors a nationwide breeder referral service for all AKC-recognized breeds. You can find this information on the AKC web site (www.akc.org) or by calling them.

Advertisements

What about classified ads? Some national dog periodicals, such as *Dog World* and *Dog Fancy*, have many ads for purebred dogs. Your local newspaper may have ads for Dachshund puppies. Because these publications cannot screen their advertisers, you must be cautious. Beware of ads that list several different breeds or "rare" colors. These may be breeders who are interested only in breeding dogs to make money and who do not care about the quality of the dogs they breed. Often these dogs are poor examples of the breed. They may have been raised in less than adequate conditions and may have health problems.

What about pet shops? This is the first place that comes to the minds of many people when they are contemplating buying a puppy. They are good places to buy dog supplies and other pet-related items. They are not the place to buy a puppy, as the selection of puppies is not of the highest caliber. Responsible breeders do not sell to pet shops; they would not want their carefully planned, nurtured, and loved puppies to go to an uncertain fate.

Meeting a Responsible Breeder

Your first contact with a breeder is an important one. Usually it's by telephone. This initial conversation is a good way for each of you to gain information about the other. Tell the breeder why you want a Dachshund. Ask how many puppies are available, their age, their sex, and, if it's important to you, their color.

Ask whatever you want to know about the breed, as well. Responsible breeders will spend time answering your questions, especially regarding care, feeding, and health issues. They should be able to provide registration information, a pedigree, health records, and feeding instructions, so ask about those.

The breeder will likely have many questions for you. Don't be surprised at some of the questions you may be asked. The breeder will spend time interviewing you to determine how the puppy will be kept. You will be asked if you have any other animals, if you have children, and if so, how many and their ages. Any

Breeders care deeply about the fate of every puppy they breed, and will have a lot of questions for you.

question asked is designed to ensure the well-being of the puppy. Responsible breeders are more concerned about the welfare of the puppies they breed than about selling you a puppy, and this concern will be apparent in their discussions with you.

They will welcome a visit to their kennel or home before you commit to a purchase, and will enthusiastically show you all the dogs and puppies that they have so that you can see the type of dogs they breed. If you buy a pet-quality puppy, a reputable breeder will usually insist that you have the puppy spayed or neutered.

Responsible breeders will not hesitate to recommend another breed if they think the Dachshund is not the right breed for you. They also will not hesitate to recommend you to another responsible Dachshund breeder if they do not have the right puppy or dog for you.

Visiting the Breeder's Premises

There are several things to look for when you make your visit to the breeder's facility. Whether the breeder has a kennel building and exercise runs separate from the house, or whether dogs are kept in crates in a special place in the house with just a run or a pen on the outside is of no importance. Many responsible breeders breed only one or two litters a year and keep only a few adult dogs, so this is all they need.

Make sure the registration papers for your puppy are available when you take her home.

The most important thing about the premises in which the dogs and puppies are kept is that they should be clean. This includes the whelping box that the puppies may still use on occasion, the dog run, the yard, and the crates or pens the dogs stay in. Do not expect the breeder's home, kennel (if there is one), and grounds to look like an ad for a house and garden magazine. Taking proper care of dogs is a time-consuming task. Often there is not enough time to take care of everything that needs to be done around the house and yard, so things can get a bit cluttered. But *everything* should be clean, including the dogs.

Examining the Puppies

The puppies should be clean, healthy, outgoing babies who are bright-eyed and full of energy. Puppies who cluster in a corner, hold their tails between their legs, and seem to be afraid should be viewed with suspicion. This could be an indication of temperament problems, or it might suggest they have been raised with a minimal amount of interaction with humans.

Healthy puppies should have strong bones and solid muscles. Check their eyes and ears for any discharge or odor. Lift the hair to see if the skin is free of sores, scales, and parasites. Ask to see health certificates that show which inoculations have been given to the pups and which ones are due, as well as information that says if the puppies have been wormed.

Personality Types

Even though good breeding and a puppy's early environment have an impact on her overall temperament, puppies, like people, have their own individual personalities. When studying a puppy you might like to take home, look for characteristics that are indicators of her particular personality.

If a puppy withdraws from or avoids contact with people, this could be a shy or timid puppy. Eventually this puppy will probably become comfortable with you, but most likely she will always have a fear of strangers and unfamiliar surroundings and situations, and will display her insecure nature by reverting to this withdrawal behavior. Puppies who have this type of personality should not be considered if you have children. A puppy of this kind does best with an owner who makes few demands and who has a quiet lifestyle.

At the other end of the scale is the puppy who is so outgoing and independent that she is overbearing. This individual may constantly demand a lot of attention and may not be the easiest dog in the world to train or control. A dog with this type of personality can be taxing on those who live with her and is usually not a good choice for a first-time dog owner or a family with children.

Puppies who are adventurous and inquisitive will most likely be outgoing individuals who are pleasant and fun to be with. They will be the ones who retain their loving characteristics but still offer a challenge to their owners—which is why they are so much fun! Fortunately, most Dachshunds who are bred and raised by serious, responsible breeders who provided them with the best possible environment will have this type of personality.

Different pups have different personalities. Some will be very outgoing, while others might be more wary with strangers.

When Is She Ready to Come Home?

No puppy should be less than 8 weeks old when you bring her home. Puppies learn their first lessons in behavior from socializing with their littermates and their mother. Puppies taken from their canine family too soon feel abandoned and miss the warmth and comfort of their siblings and mother. This can cause many sleepless nights for the new owners, because these are generally the puppies that cry all night. It is also important that puppies be fully weaned and are strong enough to be on their own.

My personal opinion is that a puppy should be about 3 months when she goes to a new home. At this age she will have her permanent immunizations. She can usually adjust more readily to a new environment, can be more easily housetrained, and is old enough to begin to learn basic training principles.

All of these suggestions apply to puppies of all coat varieties, colors, and sizes. In the first chapter, if you remember, there was some discussion regarding certain personality differences in each coat variety. Keep those in mind when looking at prospective puppies.

What About an Adult Dachshund?

Up to this point, the focus has been on choosing a puppy. There's no doubt a young puppy is adorable, but don't rule out an older puppy or an adult dog. Depending on your circumstances, an older puppy or an adult may be a better choice for you. Older puppies give a more accurate picture of what they will be like as adults in regard to size and looks. At an older age, the activity level, the personality, and overall soundness of a dog can be more easily determined.

There are many advantages to getting an adult dog. They have outgrown the destructiveness and rambunctiousness of puppyhood and are generally calmer. More than likely they are housetrained and probably have received some basic training. These factors can be quite important, especially if the person acquiring the dog is older and an energetic puppy may be too much to handle. Perhaps you do not have enough time to devote to a new puppy, but you would be able to give an adult dog what she needs.

Breeders may have older puppies and adult dogs who could use a good home. Don't be concerned that an adult will not adjust to her new environment or come to love you. Dachshunds are devoted and loving by nature, and they readily transfer their devotion and love to their new owner.

Adult Dachshunds can make great pets, and will form a close bond with you.

Rescue Dachshunds

You may want to consider getting a Dachshund from a rescue group or a humane society. The unfortunate dogs (both adults and puppies) are, for whatever reason, no longer wanted by their owners. Most of these Dachshunds can make good pets for someone who will give them a loving home.

There are Dachshund rescue groups in almost every part of the country. They are usually affiliated with and sponsored by local Dachshund clubs. The people who work with rescue groups are caring volunteers who love dogs. They are as careful and thorough in placing rescue dogs as are responsible breeders.

It should be understood that these dogs are not available to just anyone who expresses a desire to have a Dachshund. Most rescue organizations have guidelines about who is eligible to adopt a rescue dog. More than likely they will have a standard application for the interested party to fill out. If the applicant meets the criteria for an adoption, an adoption agreement or contract is generally required. The purpose of these guidelines is to make sure the dog is never homeless again.

Your Life with Your Dachshund Begins

Once you have found the puppy or dog you feel is the right one for you, she becomes a part of your life. You and your Dachshund are about to begin a relationship that will last for her lifetime. From the moment you take your dog into your home, your life will never be the same. I guarantee that the experience will enrich your life beyond any of your expectations.

Part II

Caring for Your Dachshund

Chapter 5

Bringing Your Dachshund Home

Now the adventure begins! You should be prepared for your Dachshund puppy or adult dog *before* you bring him into your home. If you have made the necessary preparations, you and your new family member will both be happier. This is particularly true if your new addition is a puppy. Puppies can be a real challenge. If you have owned a dog before, you probably have a pretty good idea of what to expect. If you are a first-time dog owner, you may be in for quite a surprise.

Before picking up your puppy, a responsible breeder has probably given you a list of items you'll need. You'll also find a basic shopping list on page 54.

Where to Keep Your Puppy

In addition to your shopping trip to the pet supply store, you also need to give some thought to where the puppy will stay during the day and where he will sleep at night. The most important things to keep in mind are keeping the puppy safe and preventing the destruction of household items such as carpeting and furniture. Dachshund puppies are no different from any other puppy: They have a natural curiosity that often leads them into trouble. For this reason, the place you select should be as safe and as immune to damage as possible.

Where you decide to keep your puppy is purely a personal decision based on the layout of your home and your tolerance level for the problems that will invariably arise until your puppy is trained, has matured, and is ready to be allowed free run of the house. The kitchen is a popular choice for a puppy pen, but any uncarpeted and relatively furniture-free area will do. You'll need to block off the doorways with sturdy baby gates or enclose a specific area with a portable dog pen. Make sure the gates are fastened securely and that they or a pen is high enough that there is no possibility your puppy can climb over. Also be sure your puppy won't be able to slip underneath or through the barriers. There are many baby gates on the market today, and some even unlatch so you can pass through and still keep the puppy confined.

If the puppy will be free in the kitchen, make sure all wires, cords, and cables are well out of reach. Be certain there is nothing on low shelves that he can get into and no spaces between or behind cabinets or appliances where he could conceivably get stuck. Remember, the Dachshund is *curious!*

Make sure, if you have children, that toys or pieces of games or puzzles are out of reach. Puppies put everything into their mouths! Cleaning supplies stored underneath cabinets that could be opened by an inquisitive nose, medicine, aerosol cans, tools, and especially plastic garbage bags are potential hazards. Plastic bags can mean death to all animals and children—small pieces torn off can block the windpipe and cause suffocation. You'll find more puppy-proofing tips on pages 56–57.

Think hard about where in the house you will keep your puppy, remembering that he is small and curious about everything.

Puppy Essentials

You'll need to go shopping *before* you bring your puppy home. There are many, many adorable and tempting items at pet supply stores, but these are the basics.

- **Food and water dishes.** Look for bowls that are wide and low or weighted in the bottom so they will be harder to tip over. Stainless steel bowls are a good choice because they are easy to clean (plastic never gets completely clean) and almost impossible to break. Avoid bowls that place the food and water side by side in one unit—it's too easy for your dog to get his water dirty that way.
- **Leash.** A six-foot leather leash will be easy on your hands and very strong.
- **Collar.** Start with a nylon buckle collar. For a perfect fit, you should be able to insert two fingers between the collar and your pup's neck. Your dog will need larger collars as he grows up.
- **Crate.** Choose a sturdy crate that is easy to clean and large enough for your puppy to stand up, turn around, and lie down in.
- **Bed.** Beds made of any material other than metal are not practical for Dachshunds. Wicker, bamboo, or any kind of plastic beds are a definite no! These dogs *chew* on anything. To discourage this habit, a taste deterrent called Bitter Apple can be helpful. This comes in a spray and a cream. It will save your antique table legs and possibly your favorite chair.
- **Nail cutters.** Get a good, sharp pair that are the appropriate size for the nails you will be cutting. Your dog's breeder or veterinarian can give you some guidance here.
- **Grooming tools.** Different kinds of dogs need different kinds of grooming tools. See chapter 7 for advice on what to buy.
- **Chew toys.** Dogs *must* chew, especially puppies. Make sure you get things that won't break or crumble off in little bits, which the dog can choke on. Very hard plastic bones are a good choice. Dogs love rawhide bones, too, but pieces of the rawhide can get caught in your dog's throat, so they should only be allowed when you are there to supervise.
- **Toys.** Watch for sharp edges and unsafe items such as plastic eyes that can be swallowed. Many toys come with squeakers, which dogs can also tear out and swallow. All dogs will eventually destroy their toys; as each toy is torn apart, replace it with a new one.

Using a Crate

One of the most valuable items you'll buy for your new puppy or dog is a crate. I can't emphasize enough how important it is to have one. It should be one of the *first* things you buy *before* you bring your dog home. Having a crate for your Dachshund will make your life a lot easier and make your puppy's life a lot safer. It will also make housetraining much simpler and will expand your choices of where you can put your dog.

Sometimes people are shocked at the thought of crating a dog and believe it is cruel. When I was actively breeding and showing Dachshunds and would sell puppies, most new owners would visibly and verbally express their disagreement when I strongly suggested they get a crate for their puppy. It took a lot of education and reasoning to convince them that it was in their best interest, and the puppy's, to do this.

In the wild, young dogs seek the safety of their den. Your dog has retained this instinct to seek a secluded and protected niche where he can rest and feel sheltered. That niche is his crate, where he will feel safe and secure.

It is wise to have his crate open in the room when he's loose so he can get used to it. Leave a towel inside and his toys. He will go in and out at will and soon consider it his special den. Then, when you close the door, he will be in a secure, familiar place. It is a good idea to feed him in his crate and to have him spend time in his crate.

Crates come in several styles and sizes. One popular and versatile style is made of lightweight plastic with a metal grated door. It's suitable for airline travel and can be cleaned easily.

There are also crates made of sturdy metal wire, which provide more ventilation, stay cleaner, are completely collapsible, and allow your Dachshund to see everything that is going on around him. However, they are not suitable for airline travel and do not hold in the warmth in colder weather. This last point is of no concern, however, if the crate is to be used exclusively in the house. I personally prefer a wire crate for indoor use, because it enables your Dachshund to feel that he is still part of things, since he can see all around him. It also enables you to completely see your Dachshund if he has a problem while in his crate. However, these crates are not easy to transport, so if you plan to travel with your dog, you may want to get two crates—one of each type.

Your Dachshund's crate should be big enough to allow him to completely stand up, completely turn around, and comfortably lie down. If you are going to have a home crate and a traveling crate, you may want the home crate to be a little larger, since the dog will be spending most of his time in this one. A crate that is more confining is better for travel, though, because if there are sudden

Puppy-Proofing Your Home

You can prevent much of the destruction puppies can cause and keep your new dog safe by looking at your home and yard from a dog's point of view. Get down on all fours and look around. Do you see loose electrical wires, cords dangling from the blinds, or chewy shoes on the floor? Your pup will see them too!

In the kitchen:

- Put all knives and other utensils away in drawers.
- Get a trash can with a tight-fitting lid.
- Put all household cleaners in cupboards that close securely; consider using childproof latches on the cabinet doors.

In the bathroom:

- Keep all household cleaners, medicines, vitamins, shampoos, bath products, perfumes, makeup, nail polish remover, and other personal products in cupboards that close securely; consider using childproof latches on the cabinet doors.
- Get a trash can with a tight-fitting lid.
- Don't use toilet bowl cleaners that release chemicals into the bowl every time you flush.
- Keep the toilet bowl lid down.
- Throw away potpourri and any solid air fresheners.

In the bedroom:

- Securely put away all potentially dangerous items, including medicines and medicine containers, vitamins and supplements, perfumes, and makeup.
- Put all your jewelry, barrettes, and hairpins in secure boxes.
- Pick up all socks, shoes, and other chewables.

In the rest of the house:

- Tape up or cover electrical cords; consider childproof covers for unused outlets.
- Knot or tie up any dangling cords from curtains, blinds, and the telephone.

- Securely put away all potentially dangerous items, including medicines and medicine containers, vitamins and supplements, cigarettes, cigars, pipes and pipe tobacco, pens, pencils, felt-tip markers, craft and sewing supplies, and laundry products.
- Put all houseplants out of reach.
- Move breakable items off low tables and shelves.
- Pick up all chewable items, including television and electronics remote controls, cellphones, shoes, socks, slippers and sandals, food, dishes, cups and utensils, toys, books and magazines, and anything else that can be chewed on.

In the garage:

- Store all gardening supplies and pool chemicals out of reach of the dog.
- Store all antifreeze, oil, and other car fluids securely, and clean up any spills by hosing them down for at least ten minutes.
- Put all dangerous substances on high shelves or in cupboards that close securely; consider using childproof latches on the cabinet doors.
- Pick up and put away all tools.
- Sweep the floor for nails and other small, sharp items.

In the yard:

- Put the gardening tools away after each use.
- Make sure the kids put away their toys when they're finished playing.
- Keep the pool covered or otherwise restrict your pup's access to it when you're not there to supervise.
- Secure the cords on backyard lights and other appliances.
- Inspect your fence thoroughly. If there are any gaps or holes in the fence, fix them.
- Make sure you have no toxic plants in the garden.

Your dog will come to regard his crate as his safe haven.

stops or abrupt shifts, your dog will not slide around as much as he would in a bigger crate.

There are also self-contained puppy pens where the puppy can sleep on one side and still have room for newspapers on the other side, so he can relieve himself without soiling his bed. There are also exercise pens that are portable, fold up, and can be used outdoors as well. They are open on top and can be clipped with standard snap locks. You can enlarge them as your puppy requires more space.

These flexible pens make an excellent outdoor confinement area if your yard is not fenced. If you do have a fenced yard, these pens can be clipped to your existing chain link to set boundaries for your Dachshund if you do not want him to have the freedom of the entire yard or have gardens you don't want dug up and rearranged. They also come in handy if you can't watch your puppy every minute and want to be sure he's safe. The Dachshund is a dog who does not do well staked or tied outside, and a puppy should *never* be left out that way.

Your Dachshund's First Days

The big day has arrived. You are ready to bring your Dachshund home. It is a good idea to try to get your puppy or dog to relieve himself before you start on your journey. Don't be upset if your puppy gets carsick on the way home. Hopefully, his breeder will have withheld his normal meal if it was scheduled close to the time when you picked him up. In any case, be prepared, but not concerned, if the dog is carsick.

The first few weeks with your new dog are so exciting for both of you! Leaving his familiar surroundings and being with people he doesn't know in a strange place can be very frightening for a puppy, though. Try to make this experience as pleasant and comforting as possible. That is why this trip home is the one exception to the fundamental rule that your dog should be in a crate while traveling. On this one trip, have someone hold the puppy in a blanket or towel. Talk to him in a soothing and loving manner to try to make him feel as secure as possible.

The arrival of your new family member is an exciting time for everyone. Keep in mind, though, that your puppy will probably be feeling confused and somewhat frightened. If there are children in the family, be sure they have been well prepared for the dog's arrival. They must learn how to behave around a dog and how to handle him properly, particularly if he's a puppy. Above all, they must be taught that a dog isn't a toy. Children must learn to be gentle while the dog is getting used to them and they are getting used to the dog.

It is best to take your Dachshund puppy to the area you have set up for him. Put him on the floor and let him explore his new surroundings. Have his water dish filled with water and offer him some. Sit on the floor and let your puppy come to you. If there are other family members present, have them do the same

Your Dachshund will learn the house rules from you, but until he does, giving him free run of the house is just inviting trouble.

thing. Puppies are inquisitive and will probably check everyone out. When you can see that he realizes he is not in any danger, you can begin to pick him up slowly and gently. The most important thing is to go slowly. Remember, your puppy has no idea of what to expect. If you use this gradual approach, it won't be long before your puppy will begin to feel comfortable with you and his new family.

Depending on his age, your puppy's first night is likely to be a disturbing one for your family. The younger your puppy is, the more probable it is that he will be confused and frightened at being away from his mother and his littermates. He will let you know this by loud, mournful wails that can last for a remarkably long time. This is a perfect example of the usefulness of a crate. If you put him in his crate beside your bed, he will probably be quiet during the night, because he is reassured by your presence. If you leave him in a room by himself, he will cry and howl and you will have to steel yourself to ignore his heartbreaking cries. You might try putting a loud ticking clock with him. Sometimes a radio playing softly will also help. Regardless of what room in the house he is in, it is always strongly recommended that you crate your puppy or dog for the night, to keep him safe.

For the first few days, your puppy will most likely experience some form of separation anxiety at leaving his mother and littermates. This anxiety can be significantly reduced if you plan your time so that for the first three or four days you or someone is with the puppy all day. During this introduction period, keep the puppy involved with plenty of attention from family members.

If you do have children, this is a great time to teach them how to handle puppies and to explain specific, commonsense rules on how to play with them. Make them understand that these are hard and fast rules that must be followed. If you are a one-person household, then just plan to devote all your time to your puppy for several days. When someone isn't with the puppy, he will be eating, sleeping, or going to the bathroom. You will be surprised at how your devotion to your dog in these early days will hasten the housetraining and obedience training processes.

Leaving Your Puppy Home Alone

Do not feel your puppy is being deprived if you have to leave him home alone. There are ways to get him accustomed to this. I strongly advise that you crate your dog any time you leave the house. However, no dog should be crated for more than about six hours at a time, and puppies must be let out much more frequently for potty breaks (see chapter 10). If you are going to be gone a long time, you should make arrangements for someone to come over and let your puppy out to relieve himself and get a little exercise. As your Dachshund gets older, he can stay in his crate for longer periods of time.

Lots of attention and gentle, supervised play will help your puppy adjust to his new home.

Especially for a puppy, it is wise to have a radio on, tuned to a talk or classi-
cal music station. The continuous sounds will soothe your puppy and keep him
company.

Get into the habit of telling your puppy or dog that he's to be a good boy
while you are away, and that you'll be back. If you have time, warm up the car,
then pop back into the house to tell him he's a good boy and that you will be
back. Repeat "be a good boy" and "I'll be back" each time you leave the house.
In a very short time, he will realize that you will indeed return.

Chapter 6

Feeding Your Dachshund

One of the things you must remember when dealing with a Dachshund is that most of them will eat almost anything, anytime, anywhere. And they will keep eating as long as food is available. There may be a few individual dogs who are picky eaters or who walk away from their food dish with some food left—but that's not the norm. More often than not, a Dachshund will polish off her own meal and then try to con you into giving her anything that you happen to be eating. She will be persistent, so you *must be firm*.

A proper diet, which includes always having fresh water available, is essential to keeping your Dachshund healthy and happy. There are basic nutrients that your dog needs. These are the same ones you need: proteins, carbohydrates, fats, minerals, and vitamins. It is essential that the food you feed your Dachshund contains all of these nutrients, in the right amounts and proportions.

Finding the Right Food

Most premium commercial dog foods sold today will meet your dog's nutritional needs, and are probably more properly balanced and nutritionally sound than the food we eat! It is best to start with the brand of food the breeder of your Dachshund was using. You may want to change at a later time, but at the beginning you should continue feeding a puppy, or an adult dog, what she has been used to eating. Abrupt changes in food can often lead to digestive upsets or, most likely, diarrhea.

Anytime in your dog's life that you decide to change her diet, do it gradually. Mix a small portion of the new food with the food she has been eating. Do this for several days. If this change does not bother her, keep adding a bit more of the new food every few days until you are now giving her about one-fourth of the old food and three-fourths of the new food. After she has been on this combination for a few days, feed only the new diet. If you are switching to a new diet for a specific health reason, the results of changing to a different food will not be readily apparent. It may take some time before you notice any significant change in your Dachshund.

Commercial Dog Foods

Do the bags of dog food in the grocery store provide proper nutrition? All dog foods have an ingredients panel and a guaranteed analysis of the food printed on the label. What do these labels tell us and how can they help us to make a choice? The box on page 66 explains the basic items you'll find on a dog food label. But there's more to consider.

The major pet food companies have done extensive research to produce nutritionally sound products. Many of these reputable name brand dog foods are sold in the grocery store at a moderate price. Premium foods are sold in pet supply stores and sometimes through veterinarians' offices. These tend to be more expensive, but you do get what you pay for. The main difference between the premium foods and the brands found in the grocery store is the density per volume. In other words, a tablespoon of premium food is likely to contain more

With dog food, you generally get what you pay for. The premium foods really are better.

digestible, absorbable nutrients than a tablespoon of non-premium food, which means your Dachshund can eat a smaller amount of premium food to be well-nourished. So the higher cost of the premium food is made up in savings on the amount served. (And there is not as much to clean up later, because your dog processes the more digestible nutrients more efficiently.) Besides these factors, some veterinarians believe the higher quality ingredients in premium foods may contribute to a healthier life as the dog ages.

Avoid generic and grocery store brand dog foods, even though they are not as expensive as the premium and name brand foods. The labels on some generic foods may state that the contents are complete and balanced, but the food's nutritional benefits have not necessarily been tested on dogs in the same way the premium and brand-name foods have been. That means you don't really know what the food is doing for (or to) your dog.

There may be times when your Dachshund needs to be on a special diet. Pet food companies have developed special diets for special needs. There are therapeutic diets for dogs suffering from allergies, kidney disease, obesity, and other health problems. Your veterinarian will advise you when your Dachshund might benefit from a special diet.

What Type of Food Is Best?

Puppies should be fed a dry, hard kibble formulated specifically for puppies. If the puppy is under 3 months of age, you may want to soak the dry food in a small amount of water for a few minutes. By 3 months, most puppies can handle dry food quite well. If your pup is still having a problem, try lightly moistening the dry kibble by running water over it and draining it immediately. The kibble is then slightly damp, but is still crunchy and must be chewed.

Dry food is recommended over canned or moist dog food because the friction from chewing the dry food helps clean the dog's teeth, as well exercising the teeth and gums, which is important during the puppy's teething phase. In addition, if you read the labels on canned foods, you'll discover that many of them contain mostly fillers (rice and grains) and water. If you really feel the need to add something to the kibble, select a canned food with less filler and less moisture. Even better, add some fresh vegetables or cottage cheese to the dog's diet.

What about feeding table scraps? A diet of table scraps is unhealthy for your dog and will most likely provide an unbalanced diet. Contrary to popular belief, dogs do *not* need variety in their diet. The same food each day will not bore them.

However most dog owners, myself included, seem to have a need to give their dogs something special from time to time. So if you have some leftovers that you think your dog might enjoy, you can save them and add them to your dog's food at his meal time. A little something from the table is all right on occasion, but shouldn't become a regular routine. Be sure the food is not too rich and feed only a small amount.

Always put table scraps or extra bits of food in the dog's food dish or add them to his regular meal. Do not feed table scraps or give him bits of food while you are eating at the table. Doing so will encourage your Dachshund to beg at the table. This behavior can become a real nuisance.

> ### C A U T I O N
>
> #### No Bones
>
> Do not give your dog bones! They can splinter or shatter and the pieces can become lodged in your dog's throat. There's even a chance they may splinter and puncture the intestinal tract. This usually requires surgery and can be fatal.

Generally, it is not necessary to add vitamins to your Dachshund's meals because a good commercial dog food is balanced and complete. When I was breeding and showing dogs, I always added a multivitamin supplement and a coat conditioner to my dogs' regular diet. However, this was many years ago and commercial dog foods were not as nutritionally balanced as they are today. I do not add supplements today and my Dachshunds are thriving. Before you consider supplementing your Dachshund's diet, consult your veterinarian.

A Sensible Feeding Schedule

How often should you feed your Dachshund? By the time you bring your puppy home, she will probably be old enough that three meals will suffice: in the morning, at midday, and in the evening. If no one is at home for the noon meal, try to get a neighbor or friend to come in and give your puppy this meal. If that is not possible, you may add a little more food to the morning and evening meals.

By the time your puppy is 6 months old, two meals a day are fine until she is 1 year old. After your dog is a year old, she can be fed once a day. Some people prefer to continue to feed their Dachshund twice a day; I am one of those people. It probably matters more to me than it does to my Dachshunds that they eat twice a day, but they seem very happy with the routine and that is all that matters to me! If your dog gets just one meal a day, it is a good idea to give her a dog biscuit or two during the day to tide her over.

Whether you feed one or two meals, only leave your dog's food out for the amount of time it takes her to eat it. A minimum amount is about ten minutes. Don't leave food in her bowl for longer than thirty minutes. Always discard all the leftovers and give her fresh food at her next meal. Don't worry if your dog doesn't finish all her dinner in the allotted time. She'll quickly learn that she should. With a Dachshund, however, it is highly unlikely that she will leave even a crumb!

Reading Dog Food Labels

Dog food labels are not always easy to read, but if you know what to look for they can tell you a lot about what your dog is eating.

- The label should have a statement saying the dog food meets or exceeds the American Association of Feed Control Officials (AAFCO) nutritional guidelines. If the dog food doesn't meet AAFCO guidelines, it can't be considered complete and balanced, and can cause nutritional deficiencies.
- The guaranteed analysis lists the minimum percentages of crude protein and crude fat and the maximum percentages of crude fiber and water. Puppy food should be 26 to 28 percent protein, which is adequate for stable growth. Fat should be around 17 percent for proper absorption of nutrients and good skin and coat. The fiber content should be under 5 percent.
- A good maintenance dog food for adults will contain about 20 to 24 percent protein, about 12 percent fat, and just under 5 percent fiber. Diets higher in protein and fat are needed only if a dog takes a lot of exercise every day.
- The ingredients list the most common item in the food first, and so on until you get to the least common item, which is listed last.
- Look for a dog food that lists an animal protein source first, such as chicken or poultry meal, beef or beef byproducts, and that has other protein sources listed among the top five ingredients. That's because a food that lists chicken, wheat, wheat gluten, corn, and wheat fiber as the first five ingredients has more chicken than wheat, but may not have more chicken than all the grain products put together.
- Other ingredients may include a carbohydrate source, fat, vitamins and minerals, preservatives, fiber, and sometimes other additives purported to be healthy.
- Some grocery store brands may add artificial colors, sugar, and fillers—all of which should be avoided.
- Most foods are designed to meet the needs of a dog at a particular stage of life. Check the label to see if the food is for a puppy, an adult, or a senior dog. Your puppy should be on a puppy or growth food until she is 1 year old.

How much you feed your Dachshund depends on her individual needs. Recommended food amounts are listed on the dog food bag. Start with the amount of food listed on the bag and divide it by the numbers of meals per day to determine how much to give at each meal. But always remember that these are only guidelines; the quantity of food you give to your dog may have to be adjusted according to her individual requirements.

Puppies are growing rapidly and need to eat as much as they will eat. They will usually leave some food if they've had enough. Be observant. If your puppy is in good weight and is growing steadily, she is eating the right amount of food. If you notice that your puppy (or your adult dog) is gaining too much weight, feed her less. Fat puppies may be cute, but too much weight can hinder normal growth and development. Obesity in adults leads to many health problems.

Self-feeding or free-feeding (when food is available all the time) is not good for puppies or adult dogs. This leisurely approach to meals can encourage finicky eating. It also makes housetraining difficult. Dogs need to eat at scheduled times so that you can be more certain when they need to eliminate.

Stick to the Routine

Your Dachshund is a creature of habit, and she likes her meals in the same place and at the same time, thank you! Establish a regular time and a regular place to feed your Dachshund. Whatever time that best suits your schedule is fine, as long as you stick to the plan. An irregular eating schedule can affect your dog's digestive system and may ultimately cause chronic digestive disorders.

If your Dachshund's feeding schedule is suddenly changed, don't be surprised if she still craves a meal

Begging can be a problem with Dachshunds.

at her old feeding time. Your dog is conditioned to expect a meal at a specific time, so her internal alarm clock still produces a hunger drive. Dogs don't easily adjust to a time zone change or to daylight saving time. To prepare your dog for a time change, gradually adjust her eating schedule over a few weeks. If you forget her dinner hour—she'll remind you. She may even escort you to the cabinet where her food is stored.

How much food your dog needs will depend on her size and activity level.

I strongly suggest that you feed your dog in her crate. When you eat your meal she can also eat hers, and then rest in her crate until your meal is finished. This will eliminate begging at the table. It also provides a structured routine for you to take her outside to relieve herself as soon as she leaves her crate.

What About Treats?

Dachshunds love treats and people love to give them to their dogs. Treats are definitely valuable in the early stages of training your dog, but too many treats can upset her balanced diet and cause her to become overweight. Just as with people, snacking all day adds up to a lot of calories. I've heard so many people whose Dachshunds are overweight say, "But I feed her only once a day." They completely discount all the treats they have given the dog throughout the day. Like all good things, treats should be given in moderation.

All kinds of commercially prepared treats are available. There are dog biscuits in all sizes, from very large to very small, and all the sizes in between. Some are satisfyingly crunchy and help to scrape tartar off teeth. Others are chewy treats made of rawhide, soft-moist treats, and dog cookies that come in fun flavors and are often made with healthful ingredients such as whole wheat flour. The choices are endless.

Along with commercially prepared treats, people food can be a treat as well. As long as the food is healthy for your dog, your Dachshund will likely enjoy almost anything you give her. Bits of lean cooked meat, green beans, carrots, bits of apple, banana, and a peeled section of orange are healthy treats for your dog. My first

Dachshund loved raw carrots. When I peeled carrots, she would come running into the kitchen, dance around my feet, and make her "please give me some" sounds.

The important thing to keep in mind is to give your dog only a few small pieces of her special treat. Giving her too much will probably cause diarrhea.

A word of caution about onions: Onions can cause hemolytic anemia, a condition in which red blood cells are destroyed. Be very careful to make sure your dog doesn't eat any onions or anything that has onions as an ingredient.

Remember that chocolate is a real danger to dogs, as well. Chocolate contains a stimulant called theobromine that can make a dog seriously ill. It should be regarded as a poison for dogs. How toxic it can be depends on the size of the dog and the amount eaten, but it has and will continue to kill dogs who eat too much. *Never* give anything that has chocolate in it to your Dachshund. Please make sure your children and your guests understand this as well. If your dog gets into something that contains chocolate, watch her very closely. If she shows any signs of being sick, contact your veterinarian immediately.

Keep in mind that everything your dog eats has to count as part of her total caloric intake, so if you give her several treats a day or are adding something to her meal, you have to adjust the amount of kibble you feed her accordingly. Dachshunds should not carry extra weight. If you look down at your Dachshund and her midsection resembles a football or a basketball, you definitely need to cut down on her food!

An overweight dog is not healthy. Count the treats you feed your dog each day, and subtract that from her ration of dog food.

Chapter 7

Grooming Your Dachshund

Regular, proper grooming is important to keeping your Dachshund looking his best, as well as keeping him comfortable and contributing to his overall sense of well-being. The Dachshund is a relatively low-maintenance dog, but that doesn't mean he doesn't need grooming. In general, though, most of his grooming can be done at home.

Caring for the Smooth Coat

Let's start with the easiest variety first. The smooth Dachshund has a short, thick, shiny coat that requires very little grooming to keep him looking his best. He should be brushed often to keep his skin healthy and his coat lustrous.

The brush that is best suited for the smooth coat is a soft natural bristle brush, which is good for stimulating his skin and spreading the natural oils that help keep his coat shiny and his skin healthy. Some people prefer to use a hound glove instead of a brush. This is a grooming tool that fits on the hand like a glove. The cloth has soft bristles or rubber nubs sewn into it. Stroking your dog with the glove captures loose hair and helps stimulate the skin's natural oils. Dogs usually enjoy being groomed with a hound glove because they like the feeling that they are being petted. So while your Dachshund is lying next to you on the floor or the sofa, you can kill two birds with one stone: Give him extra attention and groom him at the same time!

The smooth coat is certainly the easiest to groom.

If you prefer a brush, by all means use it. It accomplishes the same thing. If you brush him just a little each day, your Dachshund won't even realize he's being groomed—especially if you begin when he's a young puppy.

In addition to routine brushing, you may occasionally rub a small amount of baby oil on your hands and apply it lightly to his coat to add sheen and luster. See how easy it is to make a smooth Dachshund really shine!

Caring for the Longhair Coat

The longhair coat is rather long and silky, and needs frequent and more aggressive grooming than the smooth if you want to keep your longhair Dachshund looking his best. Of course, you will brush and comb him often to remove dead hair and undercoat and to keep his coat in good condition. Bathe him regularly, but not overly frequently, and always follow the bath with a coat conditioning rinse.

If left ungroomed, the longhair coat can become thick and unkempt looking. When this happens, the dog loses his look of elegance as well as his overall body shape. He may look more like a mass of hair with a head at one end and a tail at the other. Grooming retains and enhances his elegant appearance and defines his overall Dachshund body shape. If you don't work on his coat at least every

Basic Supplies

Here are some general supplies you will need, regardless of the coat your dog has:

Bath mat
Canine nail clipper
Canine nail file
Cotton balls
Ear-cleaning solution or ear wipes
Flea comb
Grooming table (optional)
Rubber mat (optional)
Rubbing alcohol
Shampoo and conditioner specifically formulated for dogs
Soft-bristle toothbrush
Toothpaste made specifically for dogs

other day, it will mat and tangle and your task will be unpleasant for your dog and a chore for you!

If possible, take your dog to a Dachshund breeder, to someone who has a longhair and knows something about grooming, or to a professional groomer before you try grooming your longhaired Dachshund yourself. Reading descriptions of how to do it is helpful, but there is nothing like actually seeing how it is done by an experienced individual. In addition to demonstrating the techniques, someone who is knowledgeable about grooming can give you advice about the special grooming tools you will need. After you have seen a good demonstration using the proper tools, you can refer back to the explanation in this book to refresh your memory.

Using a grooming table makes grooming a Dachshund a bit easier. This special table has a rubber surface for firm footing, and it does save your back. Grooming tables are sturdy, and they can be easily folded and stored when not in use. There are grooming tables that come with an arm attached so you can leash the dog to keep him still. *Never leave your dog on the grooming table unattended (with or without the arm).* If he decides to jump down, he could hurt himself.

You can use any table for grooming, as long as it is steady and you provide a rubber or skidproof surface so your dog can have proper footing. However, unless your Dachshund has had some obedience training and ample time to accept grooming, not having a grooming table arm could be a problem.

The pin brush is an efficient tool for this type of coat. It will go deep into the undercoat as well as the surface, and will help prevent tangling.

Routinely combing your dog's coat all over with a flea comb or other fine-tooth comb will remove dead hair, which will help keep him looking tidy. When you use the brush or the comb on your longhair, go in the natural direction of the hair. You want the coat flat, not curled or wavy.

A stripping knife is also quite useful to keep your dog looking neat. This grooming tool has a very fine serrated edge and can be used like a comb. It will remove a remarkable amount of dead hair and undercoat without affecting the longer outer coat. Because of the very fine edge of this implement, go slowly and keep the skin taut in the area where you are working. It is possible for the fine edges to catch in a small fold of skin. Combing the back of the neck and the body with the stripping blade regularly will keep the longhair coat in good condition.

Before you begin to brush, use your fingers to feel for mats and tangles, especially in the armpit area and in the feathering on the legs. You need to work the tangles out before you begin combing. There are products on the market that, when soaked into the tangles, will soften them so you can undo them gently with your fingers. Combing them out before undoing them will cause your dog a great deal of discomfort.

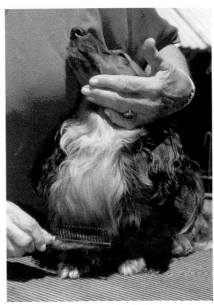

If you regularly groom your longhair, mats will not be a problem.

It is important to keep the excess hair between the toes and on the bottoms of the feet trimmed, because this hair is a natural trap for dirt and debris. The hair on the bottom of the feet should be cut with a pair of straight scissors so that it is even with the pads. With blunt-edged scissors, trim around the edges of each foot to give the foot a round, compact look. You may have to trim the top of the foot around the nails to remove fluffy hairs that may stick up over the nails.

If there is a lot of hair on the underside of the tail in the anal area, this should be trimmed so he won't soil himself when he defecates. To do this, hold his tail straight out from the base. Using the blunt-edged scissors, keep the tail extended with one hand, and scissor the excess with the other hand from the base out about an inch or more.

Caring for the Wirehair Coat

As previously suggested for the longhair, take your dog to a breeder, to someone who has a wirehair and knows something about grooming them, or to a professional groomer before you try grooming your dog yourself. There is nothing like actually seeing how it is done. Again, the experts can advise you about the type of tools you'll need to keep your dog looking his best.

Even if you are not going to show your wirehair, it is helpful to understand the look you are trying to achieve when you groom him. According to the

The wirehair should have a uniform, tight, short, rough coat.

description in the Dachshund standard, the whole body of the wirehair is covered with a perfectly uniform, tight, short, thick, rough, hard coat that has finer short hairs, called the undercoat, distributed everywhere between the coarser long hairs. The exceptions are the jaw, eyebrows, and ears; there should be a beard on the chin and the eyebrows should be bushy. The hair on the ears should be shorter than on the body, but still conform to the rest of the coat. The goal in grooming a wirehair is to enhance the Dachshund body outline and emphasize the characteristics of the wire coat.

> **TIP**
>
> **Special Tools for the Wirehair Coat**
>
> Blunt-edged (rounded) scissors
>
> Hound glove
>
> Medium-tooth comb
>
> Pin brush
>
> Stripping comb
>
> Thinning shears

Wirehair coats vary greatly from the very short, thick, and harsh, which is the most desirable type, to a quite soft coat, which is not desirable if you are interested in showing your dog. Of course, there are many varying degrees of coat texture in between. Just how harsh your dog's coat is will determine what tools you'll need to use. A really harsh or tight wire needs minimal care. This type of coat can be brushed with the pin brush or the hound glove.

If you begin to see the hair sticking up a little along the dog's back and your wirehair begins to look rather unkempt, you will need to use a stripping comb. A stripping comb (*never* use a razor-edged comb) is used gently down the back on a slant to thin out the guard hairs (the longer, stiffer hairs of the outercoat). Never dig into the coat, just skim on the angle. You're thinning, not cutting.

You can run a comb through your dog's beard as often as needed to keep it from tangling. If the beard or eyebrows are too long or too thick, use blunt-edged scissors to trim them.

While electric clippers should never be used in preparing a wire for the show ring, they can be used with good results on dogs who are not going to be shown. They simplify the grooming process for someone who doesn't have the time or the knowledge of how to strip or pluck. Clipping your dog is a timesaving way to keep the dog looking neat and still generally create the desired look that you want for your wirehair.

A wire with a soft coat is a good candidate for the clippers. The soft wire coat is fine and often long, and will mat and tangle. It will require much daily maintenance and will be quite time-consuming. If you have a wirehair with a soft coat, check his ears to be sure he doesn't have hair on the inside of them. If he does, gently pluck it out. Otherwise this hair becomes packed down in the ear, trapping all manner of unpleasant things—your dog can wind up with ear mites, yeast infections, and bacteria.

A soft wire coat can be clipped down short, especially during the summer months, to keep fleas and ticks under control. Perhaps you can find a breeder or groomer who will show you how to clip your wire Dachshund yourself. *Don't attempt to do this yourself if you have had no experience.* You could frighten your dog or injure him, and then grooming will be a terrifying ordeal for him for the rest of his life.

Bathing

How often you bathe your Dachshund is a matter of personal judgment. Generally, you will know when it is time to bathe your dog by the way he looks and smells. This depends on the environment he lives in and what he does. Is he primarily a house dog who only goes outdoors on a leash and is usually walked on pavement, or is he outdoors a great deal where he runs on and rolls in the grass, as well as in anything else that might be present such as dead leaves, worms, and other unmentionables? The type of coat he has is another consideration. Smooths and wires do not need to be bathed as often as longhairs.

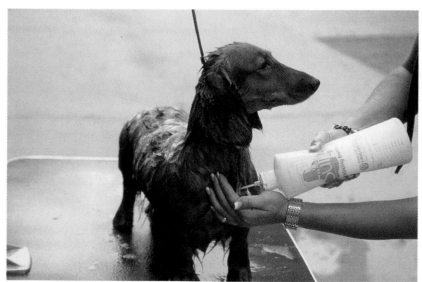

Never use your own shampoo on your dog. Human shampoos will dry out a dog's coat.

Dachshunds normally do not have a "doggy" odor, so unless your Dachshund comes into contact with something smelly, frequent bathing is not necessary. Bathing your dog too often can remove the natural oils from his coat, which are necessary to keep his coat shiny and to prevent his skin from becoming too dry, which can lead to skin problems. In general, all dogs should be bathed at least two or three times a year. Beginning with this as a bare minimum, how frequently you bathe your dog depends upon your judgment and your particular situation.

Before you bathe your Dachshund, brush him. A thorough brushing beforehand removes loose hair and significantly aids the effectiveness of the shampoo in cleaning down to the skin. It also helps lessen the amount of hair that comes out during washing and makes bathing a less hairy job.

Decide where you will bathe your dog. A large sink or laundry tub is big enough for a Dachshund. Place a rubber mat on the bottom of the sink or tub so your dog has more secure footing. You may want to put a cotton ball in his ears to prevent water from getting into the ear canals.

Dogs who are placed in a tub that already has water in it often try to scramble out and will get water everywhere. You may want to put your dog in a dry tub and then slowly add the water, or use a handheld hose attachment to wet him down. Test the water temperature before putting him in the sink or wetting him down. The water should be warm, not hot or too cold. Either extreme will make it unpleasant for your dog and might make giving future baths more difficult.

There are many dog shampoos, and the one you choose will depend on your Dachshund's coat variety and his overall skin condition. It is not wise to use shampoos made for humans. They contain harsher detergents, are not pH balanced for dogs, and could damage hair or sensitive skin.

Wet your dog down thoroughly and apply the shampoo. Use a wet washcloth or sponge to wash his head, ears, and muzzle. Be careful not to get shampoo in his eyes.

Rinse your dog completely (a handheld hose attachment makes this a lot easier), paying particular attention to the groin area, armpits, and between the toes. Be certain no shampoo residue is left behind. This will cause dryness, flaking, and itching of your dog's skin. For smooths and longhairs, follow the rinsing with a good quality conditioner, which will make your dog's coat soft and shiny. Do not use conditioners with the tight-coated wire; you do not want a soft coat here. Conditioners made especially for dogs are available at pet supply stores or can be ordered through pet supply catalogs.

Towel dry your dog, removing as much moisture from his coat as you can. The first thing your Dachshund will want to do after his bath is shake himself, which is why it is important to absorb as much water from his coat as you can with the towel. After he has completed all the shaking that he feels is necessary, continue towel drying him. Towel dry your smooth briskly, your wirehair with flat strokes so as not to ruffle his coat, and your longhair with the towel draped to keep the coat flat. If your dog is not afraid of it, you may use a hair dryer on all coats to complete the drying process. Do not let your dog go outdoors until his hair is completely dry, especially if it is cold outside.

If you notice that your Dachshund's skin is dry and flaking, or that your longhaired Dachshund's coat is dry, brittle, curly, or wavy, apply baby or bath oil to his coat and brush it in thoroughly *before* the bath. Leave it on for a few hours, bathe, and then follow his bath with a good quality conditioner. While his coat is still damp, put a dry towel over his back and pin it securely at the chest and under his belly. Keep him in a warm place, away from drafts until his coat is thoroughly dry. Remove the towel and brush his coat. Do not use a hair dryer when skin is dry and flaking.

Ears, Eyes, and Teeth

Check your Dachshund's ears every week. A healthy ear will look clean and will not give off any unpleasant odors. Normal ears may have a slight amount of waxy buildup in the external ear. You can clean the surface inside the earflap and *only* the part of the ear canal that you see by using cotton balls dipped in alcohol or cotton applicator swabs with a special ear-cleansing solution. Ear cleaning wipes are also available.

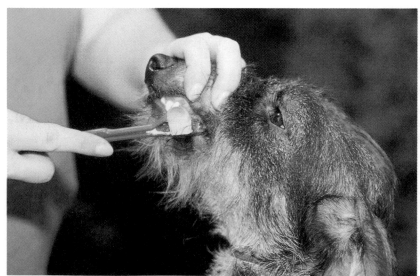

Brushing your dog's teeth regularly will help avoid expensive veterinary dental procedures later in life.

Your Dachshund does not have a safe, effective way of keeping his eyes clean. Rubbing against carpeting or furniture, or trying to remove mucus buildup with paws that have nails, are ineffective and unsafe ways to keep this critical area clean. Be sure to keep your dog's eyes clear of mucus at all times. Infections are often caused by bacteria that overgrow on mucus. Use a sterile eyewash and eye wipes to keep the eye area clean.

Plaque and tartar on your dog's teeth can cause unpleasant mouth odors, tooth discoloration, and even premature loss of teeth. Routine cleaning of your Dachshund's teeth will help keep plaque and tartar from building up. Clean them using a toothpaste made especially for dogs (toothpaste for humans can be dangerous for dogs), applied with a small toothbrush or a scrap of terry cloth or gauze wrapped around your finger and rubbed over each tooth.

Nail Trimming

You must trim your dog's nails regularly. Trimming your Dachshund's nails is not just something you do to improve his appearance—it is vital for your dog's health and comfort. Long nails cause your dog's feet to splay, which leaves room for debris and small stones to get between the footpads. Overly long nails can also cause your dog pain when he walks. Dachshunds have compact feet that are designed for going through rough terrain while trailing game. To keep his feet in good order, having short nails is imperative. Even if your Dachshund doesn't do field work and is a house pet, long nails might scratch the furniture or catch in clothing, rugs, bedding, or upholstery.

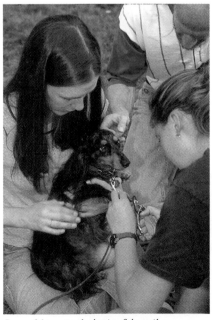

If you are uneasy about trimming your Dachshund's nails on your own, have your veterinarian, a groomer, or an experienced dog owner show you how to do it before you attempt it yourself. These experts also can be helpful in recommending, and perhaps demonstrating, the various nail trimming

Be careful to cut only the tip of the nail.

Making Your Environment Flea Free

If there are fleas on your dog, there are fleas in your home, yard, and car, even if you can't see them. Take these steps to combat them.

In your home:

- Wash whatever is washable (the dog bed, sheets, blankets, pillow covers, slipcovers, curtains, etc.).
- Vacuum everything else in your home—furniture, floors, rugs, everything. Pay special attention to the folds and crevices in upholstery, cracks between floorboards, and the spaces between the floor and the baseboards. Flea larvae are sensitive to sunlight, so inside the house they prefer deep carpet, bedding, and cracks and crevices.
- When you're done, throw the vacuum cleaner bag away—in an outside garbage can.
- Use a nontoxic flea-killing powder, such as Flea Busters or Zodiac FleaTrol, to treat your carpets (but remember, it does not control fleas elsewhere in the house). The powder stays deep in the carpet and kills fleas (using a form of boric acid) for up to a year.
- If you have a particularly serious flea problem, consider using a fogger or long-lasting spray to kill any adult and larval fleas, or having a professional exterminator treat your home.

tools. There are three basic types of trimmers: a clipper, a file, and an electric grinder.

The nail clipper is a hand-held cutting instrument that is available at most pet supply stores. A nail file for dogs is quite similar to the kind of metal nail file people use, but is designed to file a dog's nails. An electric grinder is just that: an electric grinding tool on which small, cylindrical pieces of sandpaper can be attached. When the grinder is on, the sand paper cylinder rotates at a very high speed, doing a very quick, smooth job of sanding the nails down. Grinding tools are often sold in hobby shops, and grinders for dogs are available in pet supply catalogs.

If you are going to use a clipper to trim your Dachshund's nails, you must be very careful to avoid cutting the quick, which runs down the center of the nail and contains nerves and blood vessels. If you cut into the quick, it will hurt your dog, and he'll be quite reluctant to let you continue or to ever have you trim his

In your car:

- Take out the floor mats and hose them down with a strong stream of water, then hang them up to dry in the sun.
- Wash any towels, blankets, or other bedding you regularly keep in the car.
- Thoroughly vacuum the entire interior of your car, paying special attention to the seams between the bottom and back of the seats.
- When you're done, throw the vacuum cleaner bag away—in an outside garbage can.

In your yard:

- Flea larvae prefer shaded areas that have plenty of organic material and moisture, so rake the yard thoroughly and bag all the debris in tightly sealed bags.
- Spray your yard with an insecticide that has residual activity for at least thirty days. Insecticides that use a form of boric acid are nontoxic. Some newer products contain an insect growth regulator (such as fenoxycarb) and need to be applied only once or twice a year.
- For an especially difficult flea problem, consider having an exterminator treat your yard.
- Keep your yard free of piles of leaves, weeds, and other organic debris. Be especially careful in shady, moist areas, such as under bushes.

nails again. It is difficult to see the quick on the Dachshund's nail, because the nails are black. Before you begin cutting, examine your dog's nails carefully and very gently. You will notice that your Dachshund's nail has a broad base that leads to a definite point where the nail begins to taper abruptly and curve downward. This point is where the nail should be cut. Another way to determine the location of the quick is to look under the nail. You will see a groove running from the tip toward the foot. The end of this groove is generally where the quick begins. If you cut no farther than that, you most likely will not cut into the quick.

To be on the safe side, you should always keep a container of styptic powder handy when trimming nails. If you do trim the nail a little too short and it begins to bleed, take a bit of this powder and press it on the cut end of the nail and apply gentle pressure. This powder is a coagulant and will stop the bleeding quickly. (In a pinch, a bit of cornstarch will also do.)

To avoid cutting into the quick, some people prefer to just file the nails down. However, this is a slow process when you consider how many nails you have to trim on your dog. Your Dachshund may not be willing to hold still for that long while you are working on his feet.

If you are squeamish about trimming your dog's nails, using a file in conjunction with the nail clippers can be the answer. You can cut just the tip off with the clippers, and then can finish the rest with the nail file. Not only does this lessen the chance of cutting the nail too short, but the nail file will smooth out any rough edges that are typically found on a freshly cut nail.

Using the electric grinder is the fastest way to keep your Dachshund's nails short and smooth. If you are more comfortable using this tool to do the job and are willing to pay more than a nail clipper and a file would cost, this may be your best bet. If you have more than one dog, an electric grinder is especially useful in keeping all their nails short and smooth with the least amount of time and effort.

The position your dog is in when you trim his nails should be the one that is most comfortable for you and your dog. I have found that holding my Dachshund on my lap is the most comfortable for me and my dog. Most breeders begin snipping off just the tiniest bit of the nail when the puppy's nails begin to curve and become sharp. This is generally done while holding the puppy in the lap and making him comfortable.

If your Dachshund didn't come from this kind of background, the best thing to do is begin cutting your puppy's nails early on. Hold him on your lap and play with his feet to get him used to having them touched. Rub the nail clippers across his paws but don't cut anything. Let him smell them and feel them, all the while speaking to him in soothing tones. Then gently take hold of his paw and cut barely the tip of the nail. Praise him lavishly and try not to let him pull away from you. Go slowly and stop before he starts to object. If he begins to pull away, correct him gently and do one more nail before you stop. At the end of each session, give him a treat. You can introduce the nail file and/or the electric grinder in much the same way, if those are the tools you choose.

Using a Professional Groomer

You might decide to have your longhair or wirehair groomed professionally. As with all things, use common sense. Many Dachshund owners who have longhairs or wirehairs take them to a professional groomer. Ask your veterinarian to recommend a reliable groomer in your area, or ask a friend who has their dog groomed. If your dog came from a local, reliable breeder, they can help you with grooming and may even be willing to do it for you.

You want your Dachshund to look the way he was bred to look. Even if he is not a show dog, he is a smart-looking animal and deserves to be kept well-groomed.

Fleas and Ticks

Fleas have been a common and troublesome enemy of dogs for centuries. They are usually spotted first during a grooming session, which is why they are mentioned here. In fact, regular bathing and brushing will help prevent infestations, and enable you to catch the first little flea before it becomes the parent to thousands.

The box on page 84 describes the relatively new products on the market that often solve the average flea problem completely. These are products you get from a veterinarian, so be sure to ask your vet about them. Even though these products are highly successful in eliminating fleas, it is prudent to always be vigilant, because a dog can be reinfested by fleas brought by other dogs.

These small, wingless, brown insects live and feed on your dog, but they also lay thousands of eggs in the environment. Prevention must therefore be aimed at treating both the dog and the environment. Treating the environment means killing both the adult fleas and the larvae, and should include newer products that contain IGRs. Your veterinarian can help in finding these items. Ridding your Dachshund and the environment of fleas is of utmost importance. Adult fleas can cause allergic dermatitis, tapeworms, secondary skin infections, and in extreme cases, anemia.

Ticks are a troublesome and dangerous parasite for dogs and their owners. Ticks can transmit infectious diseases, including ehrlichia, Rocky Mountain spotted fever, and Lyme disease.

Fleas can really torment your dog, and must be dealt with promptly.

New Products in the Fight Against Fleas

At one time, battling fleas meant exposing your dog and yourself to toxic dips, sprays, powders, and collars. But today there are flea preventives that work very well and are safe for your dog, you, and the environment. The two most common types are insect growth regulators (IGRs), which stop the immature flea from developing or maturing, and adult flea killers. To deal with an active infestation, experts usually recommend a product that has both.

These next-generation flea fighters generally come in one of two forms:

- **Topical treatments or spot-ons.** These products are applied to the skin, usually between the shoulder blades. The product is absorbed through the skin into the dog's system. Among the most widely available spot-ons are Advantage (kills adult fleas and larvae), Revolution (kills adult fleas), Frontline Plus (kills adult fleas and larvae, plus an IGR), K-9 Advantix (kills adult fleas and larvae), and BioSpot (kills adult fleas and larvae, plus an IGR).
- **Systemic products.** This is a pill your dog swallows that transmits a chemical throughout the dog's bloodstream. When a flea bites the dog, it picks up this chemical, which then prevents the flea's eggs from developing. Among the most widely available systemic products are Program (kills larvae only, plus an IGR) and Capstar (kills adult fleas).

Make sure you read all the labels and apply the products exactly as recommended, and that you check to make sure they are safe for puppies.

How to Get Rid of a Tick

During tick season (which, depending on where you live, can be spring, summer, and/or fall), examine your dog every day for ticks. Pay particular attention to your dog's neck, behind the ears, the armpits, and the groin.

When you find a tick, use a pair of tweezers to grasp the tick as close as possible to the dog's skin and pull it out using firm, steady pressure. Check to make sure you get the whole tick (mouth parts left in your dog's skin can cause an infection), then dab the wound with a little hydrogen peroxide and some antibiotic ointment. Watch for signs of inflammation.

Ticks carry very serious diseases that are transmittable to humans, so dispose of the tick safely. *Never* crush it between your fingers. Don't flush it down the toilet either, because the tick will survive the trip and infect another animal. Instead, use the tweezers to place the tick in a tight-sealing jar or plastic dish with a little alcohol, put on the lid and dispose of the container in an outdoor garbage can. Wash the tweezers thoroughly with hot water and alcohol.

Ticks spend a great deal of their life cycle in the environment, where they lay hundreds of eggs. They actually spend only a short amount of their life cycle obtaining a blood meal from a host. Therefore, if you encounter a tick problem in your household or kennel, it is imperative you treat the environment as well as the pet. Professional exterminators should be called to treat the environment.

You can remove a tick that is attached to your dog, but it should be done very carefully (see the box above).

Chapter 8

Keeping Your Dachshund Healthy

A healthy Dachshund is a happy Dachshund. Keeping your Dachshund healthy is your responsibility. Your dog's breeder has laid the groundwork for your Dachshund's good health by making sure the puppy received the proper inoculations, by worming the puppy (if necessary), by providing her with a high quality food, and by raising her in a clean, loving environment. Adult dogs obtained from rescue groups or shelters have been examined by a veterinarian and given the necessary inoculations. Now it is up to you to make sure your Dachshund continues to get proper and essential health care throughout her lifetime.

Like all dogs, Dachshunds are subject to problems that can affect their health. The purpose of this chapter is not to provide an exhaustive list of canine maladies, their diagnosis, and treatment, but rather to acquaint you with some of the common health problems that occur in dogs generally, and in Dachshunds in particular.

Choosing Your Dog's Veterinarian

One of the first things any dog owner needs to do is establish a working relationship with a veterinarian. After you, the most important person involved in keeping your dog in good health is your veterinarian. For this reason, it's important to choose a veterinarian carefully—choosing a vet is like choosing your own physician. This person should have the necessary credentials and a good reputation in his field, but he also should be someone with whom you have a good rapport. You should be able to communicate with him, and he should feel comfortable with you asking him questions. Your Dachshund should be at ease with him as well.

If you've never owned a dog before, you need to find a veterinarian you can trust, someone you can depend on. Turning to the classified ads in the telephone book is not the best way to find such a person. If you got your Dachshund from a reliable breeder, ask for a recommendation. Or ask relatives, friends, acquaintances, and neighbors in your area who have pets which veterinarian they use. Call businesses involved with dogs, such as kennels or groomers, and ask for their recommendations.

Its a good idea to take your new puppy or adult dog to see the veterinarian a few days after bringing her home. Besides assuring you that everything is okay, it's a good time for the vet to get to know you and your dog.

This initial visit also is a time for you to get some general information about the clinic. When is the clinic open? Are visits by appointment only? What provisions are there for emergencies? It will also give you an opportunity to see the facilities and some of the staff. If the staff is pleasant and helpful and the veterinarian

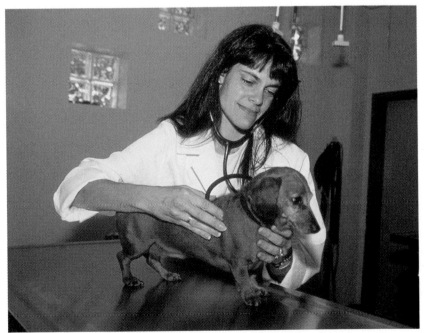

After you, your dog's veterinarian is the most important person in his life.

is considerate, caring, approachable, and someone you feel you can trust and work with, you can't ask for more than that.

If you find that you're not satisfied, you can always take your dog to another vet. Your Dachshund deserves the best health care you can provide for her. If you ever need a second opinion on a serious matter, seek one with or without your veterinarian's approval. There are specialists in all major fields of veterinary medicine. They should be consulted when necessary.

Health Concerns for Dachshunds

Certain health problems and illnesses seem to occur more frequently in Dachshunds. This does not mean every Dachshund will have every problem (or even any problem) on this list, but Dachshund owners should be aware of the health issues that are relatively common in the breed.

Obesity

Just as in humans, it is unhealthy for a dog to be overweight. Excess weight endangers the heart, lungs, and joints, and makes your Dachshund more susceptible to other ailments. It can be a factor in the development of back problems. Recent studies show a dramatic increase in the number of pet dogs who are overweight.

Dachshunds seem to be especially prone to obesity. You can prevent this problem by providing your dog with the right diet, making sure that she gets enough exercise, and refraining from giving her too many treats. Your Dachshund will live a longer, healthier, and happier life if you do.

Cushing's Disease

Cushing's disease (hyperadrenocorticism) is not uncommon in middle-aged to older Dachshunds. The basic problem is the overproduction of corticosteroids from the adrenal glands, but this is a complicated disease with a variety of causes and symptoms. The most common symptoms observed by dog owners are ravenous appetite, drinking large quantities of water, and increased urine output. Dogs with this disease often have hair loss, which results in a thin-looking coat. The skin itself may also become thin and is easily damaged and slow to heal. The abdomen becomes enlarged, giving a pot-bellied appearance. This is due to the shifting of fat to the abdomen and a weakening and wasting of muscle mass in the abdomen. Cushing's disease is more treatable than it was only a few years ago, and an oral medication is available.

Hypothyroidism

Middle-aged Dachshunds seem to be one of the many breeds predisposed to hypothyroidism, in which thyroid function falls below normal. Hypothyroidism can be the root of many complex problems and is not fully understood. The clinical signs of a hypothyroid dog are often vague and can range from mild to severe. Dogs may gain weight without an increase in appetite. They are often dull, quite lethargic, and are reluctant to exercise. They do not tolerate cold well and will seek places where they can keep warm.

Blood tests are used to diagnose hypothyroidism. Oral medication, administered daily for the rest of the dog's life, enables most dogs to lead normal lives.

Epilepsy and Seizures

Seizures can be a symptom of epilepsy, which can occur in all breeds, including mixed breeds. As a genetically transmitted trait, it can even be passed down through generations within one family. Many breeds have a tendency to develop epilepsy, and Dachshunds are one of them.

Although seizures are frequently associated with epilepsy, they can have many other causes. If your Dachshund has a seizure, don't assume she has epilepsy. A single, mild seizure is not an emergency and rarely indicates the need for long-term

Lethargy is a common sign of hypothyroidism. Medication controls the problem for most dogs.

treatment. However, you should call your veterinarian. Be sure to record the date, time, and duration of the seizure. It would be prudent to make an appointment with your veterinarian for your dog to have a thorough exam.

Epilepsy is a disorder of recurring seizures. It generally develops in dogs from 6 months to 5 years of age, but seems to occur more frequently between the ages of 2 and 3 years.

Seizures vary in intensity and duration. A mild seizure may be nothing more than a dog stiffening and then seeming to momentarily forget where she is. The dog may lose consciousness briefly, and it may look as if she just collapsed. This type of seizure is called a petite mal seizure. Grand mal seizures are more common. A dog experiencing a grand mal seizure usually falls on her side and has uncontrollable muscle activity, such as kicking her legs as if she is paddling. Salivation is profuse and often the dog involuntarily urinates and defecates. The seizure may last for a minute or more, but generally lasts about five minutes.

Seizures by themselves are not life-threatening unless they last more than twenty minutes or if your pet has one seizure right after another. Severe and long seizures are a medical emergency and can be fatal.

During the actual seizure, a dog is unaware of her surroundings so it does little good for you to try to comfort her. It is best to leave her alone. Just make sure there is nothing around on which she might hurt herself. When the dog recovers, it is good to be there to comfort her.

What triggers a seizure? This is unknown, but many dogs tend to have seizures during periods of excitability such as playing ball, when you or some other member of the family return home after being gone all day, or at the anticipation of going for a ride in the car. Some dogs have been known to have a seizure while sleeping. (Do not confuse this with dreaming. It's common for a dog to bark or shake while sleeping, but a dreaming dog can be awakened, while a dog having a seizure cannot.)

Because epilepsy can be an inherited trait, dogs who have seizures without any obvious reason, or who have developed epileptic patterns, should never be bred. If they were bred before the condition surfaced, they should immediately be removed from any breeding program.

Canine Intervertebral Disc Disease

Dachshunds have the unenviable distinction of being at the top of the list of breeds that are affected by canine intervertebral disc disease. What is this disease? Simply put, it is a back problem.

In between each vertebra of the spine is a flexible disc made of cartilage that is called an intervertebral disc. These discs provide cushioning between each

The Dachshund's long back may be one reason disc disease occurs more often in the breed.

bone and enable the neck, spine, and tail to bend, allowing changes in position and posture.

A disc that becomes weak with age or trauma may rupture, or herniate, causing a portion of the disc to protrude upward and place pressure on the spinal cord. This pressure typically prevents or inhibits nerve transmission along the spinal cord. The effect on the spinal cord will depend on the amount and severity of the pressure. Effects can include pain, weakness, and paralysis. The location of the ruptured disc also affects the spinal cord. A disc herniation in the neck area may affect the entire body, but one in the middle of the dog's back may only affect the actions of the rear legs and abdominal organs. This area is the one that is most frequently affected.

Disc problems usually manifest themselves between the ages of 2 to 5 years. The causes are not completely understood, but it is believed many factors are involved: heredity, environment, a dog's daily activities, and the structure of the breed. Surprisingly, this injury is rarely associated with severe trauma, such as being hit by a car or falling from heights. Many people believe it occurs when a Dachshund jumps off furniture or frequently goes up and down steep steps. These activities may aggravate a predisposition to the condition, but may not be the sole cause of the problem.

When a disc first ruptures, it causes intense pain. Some dogs may shiver from the pain and walk very carefully and slowly. When the rupture is severe, the back legs will be partially or completely paralyzed, either temporarily or permanently. The nerves affecting the bladder and colon may also be affected, making it difficult for the dog to urinate or defecate on her own. If the ruptured disc is in the neck, the dog will hold her head in a rigid position, and may not even want to lower it to eat and drink. She may cry when patted on the head. Whatever the symptoms, it is imperative that you seek veterinary care immediately.

Treatment varies, depending on the severity of the problem. It almost always includes the use of anti-inflammatory medications such as cortisone, which is a steroid. Painkillers such as buffered aspirin may also be used. In many cases the use of these medications along with confinement and rest, are successful in treating the problem. In severe cases, surgery is sometimes necessary to either remove the protruding disc material or cut away a portion of the bone that surrounds the spinal cord. To be most effective, however, surgery must usually be done within the first day or so following the injury.

It may take months before affected dogs heal completely. Restricting jumping activities during this period is very important in preventing reoccurrence. Consult your veterinarian about the use of a glucosamine and chondroitin nutritional supplement to help speed recovery and strengthen the damaged cartilage.

Health Concerns for All Dogs

When you look at the long list of health problems dogs can have, you must be wondering if you will be spending most of your time with your Dachshund in the veterinarian's office. This chapter is meant to inform you; your Dachshund will certainly not suffer from everything mentioned. If she does experience one or more problems, the majority of them are quite treatable.

Keeping your Dachshund healthy is a matter of prevention and common sense. A good genetic background definitely helps. Over a dog's lifetime, some health problems are likely to occur. If and when they do, you should know what to do, and have a veterinarian you have faith and confidence in to help you.

Flea Allergy Dermatitis

Sometimes called flea bite hypersensitivity, this is the most common allergy in dogs. It is seasonal, and is worse in the summer and fall—peak flea times.

Dogs will bite at the base of their tail and scratch frequently. Many will have hair loss or thinning above the base of the tail. If the dog is severely affected, she

How to Make a Canine First-Aid Kit

If your dog hurts herself, even a minor cut, it can be very upsetting for both of you. Having a first-aid kit handy will help you to help her, calmly and efficiently. I suggest these supplies be kept separate from the grooming tools and not near your family's first-aid supplies.

What should be in your canine first-aid kit?

- Antibiotic ointment
- Antiseptic and antibacterial cleansing wipes
- Benadryl
- Cotton-tipped applicators
- Disposable razor
- Elastic wrap bandages
- Extra leash and collar
- First-aid tape of various widths
- Gauze bandage roll
- Gauze pads of different sizes, including eye pads
- Hydrogen peroxide
- Instant cold compress
- Kaopectate tablets or liquid
- Latex gloves
- Lubricating jelly
- Muzzle
- Nail clippers
- Pen, pencil, and paper for notes and directions
- Pepto-Bismol
- Round-ended scissors and pointy scissors
- Safety pins
- Sterile saline eyewash
- Thermometer (rectal)
- Tweezers

may itch over her entire body, have generalized hair loss, and red inflamed skin. Hot spots are often a result of flea bite allergies.

Controlling the fleas is the most successful treatment (see chapter 7). If a dog who is on a good flea control program gets bitten and has a flare-up, antihistamines or, in severe cases, oral steroids can be used to get the itching under control.

Most canine allergies manifest themselves as itchy skin.

Food Allergies

Dogs tend to develop allergies to foods that appear most frequently in their diet. Many animals with food allergies also have concurrent inhalant or contact allergies.

Symptoms of a food allergy are similar to those of most allergies seen in dogs, with the primary sign being itchy skin. Symptoms may also include chronic or recurrent ear infections, hair loss, excessive scratching, hot spots, and skin infections that respond to antibiotics but reoccur after antibiotics are discontinued. It is difficult to distinguish food allergies from atopic dermatitis and other allergies, based solely on physical signs. Treatment begins with isolating the offending food and treating the symptoms. Your veterinarian will help you in this, and may be able to prescribe a food your dog is better able to tolerate.

Mange

Mange is a skin infestation of mites. Because these mites are not visible to the naked eye, a diagnosis is made by taking a skin scraping and examining the sample microscopically. Some of the more common mites are sarcoptes, demodex, cheyletiella, and ear mites. Because the treatment of each is different, consultation with your veterinarian is the best way to deal with a mite problem.

There are two types of mange: demodectic (follicular) and sarcoptic. In both cases, it can only be accurately detected by a veterinarian, who will administer what is needed. Dedicated, persistent treatment is absolutely essential.

Mange tends to affect puppies much more severely than it does adult dogs.

Dry Coat

Itching, visible dander or dandruff, and a lackluster appearance are all signs of a dry coat. Bathe the dog in a shampoo made for this condition. (Always use a *tear-free* shampoo on the head, near the eye region.) Shampoo from back to front, lather well, and rinse well. Repeat in ten days *if needed.*

Dry coat is more prevalent in the winter, when the heat is on and the humidity is low. You can compensate for this by adding cod liver oil to the dog's diet once or twice a week. Any oil, including vitamin E (break the capsule and add to a dog's meal), will help. Also remember that bathing too often may also deplete the natural oils in the dog's coat.

Sparse Hair and Hot Spots

Symptoms include loss of hair and small areas with no hair growth. Inflamed, hairless patches can also appear if the dog is biting or pulling at her coat or scratching.

To treat these areas, apply vitamin E oil (break the capsule) directly to the spot and rub, or apply A&D ointment to sparse areas, or add more oil to the dog's diet. Spray Bitter Apple (or a similar taste deterrent) on the coat to discourage the dog from biting or pulling at it. If none of this works, or if the spots begin to ooze or run, your dog needs veterinary care.

Ear Injuries

Trauma to the ear is usually self-inflicted by intense scratching, which can severely injure the ear. Shaking the head violently due to an ear problem can also lead to a hematoma—a blister of blood under the skin. If your Dachshund is scratching or trying to rub her ears on things like the carpet or against a chair, if she seems to be experiencing pain around the ears when you touch her, or if she is shaking her head or tilting it to one side, these are signs of an ear problem. Because dogs can have ear problems for many different reasons, it is best to contact your veterinarian to determine the cause of the problem and what secondary conditions may have resulted from it.

Any breed with hanging ears is more prone to ear infections. Regular cleaning will help prevent problems.

Ear Mites

Ear mites are one of the most common causes of ear problems in dogs. They feed on ear wax and other debris in the ear canal and can lead to intensely itchy allergic reactions, causing dogs to scratch their ears raw. They are invisible to the naked eye and are contagious to other animals. You will see the dog constantly pulling on and scratching her ears, redness in the ears, and visible debris, usually black. Ear mites require prompt veterinary attention.

Eye Discharge

This could range from debris in corner of the eye to constant tearing. Wipe the debris away with damp tissue or washcloth. If the discharge is colored, thick mucus, consult your vet. On wirehairs or longhairs, check to see if there is hair growing too close to the corner of the eye. If this is the case, pluck the hair out with your finger, having someone hold the dog's head still. If the hair is removed and the discharge continues, seek veterinary care.

Cataracts

Cataracts are a clouding of the lens of the eye. If your dog is approaching her senior years, this is a natural condition. Usually it requires no treatment—just clearing away obstacles in your home that might cause the dog harm. If this condition is noticed in a young dog, seek veterinary care. A specialist may have to be consulted.

Teeth and Gum Problems

Proper dental care is a must for your Dachshund. Studies show that by age 4, at least 80 percent of dogs exhibit signs of gum disease. These include yellow and brown buildup of tartar along gum line; red, inflamed gums; and persistent bad breath. A dog with tooth problems will rub her muzzle along chair or sofa arms, the rug, or the floor. Swelling can sometimes develop in the face area if a tooth is decaying or abscessed.

The best prevention is to clean your dog's teeth at least several times a week. If tartar does develop and is still in the early stages, you can scrape it off with a tooth scaler or even your fingernail. If tartar buildup is severe, a professional cleaning by your veterinarian is the best route to take.

Blocked Anal Glands

The anal glands are scent sacs located low down on each side of the rectum. If they become blocked, your dog may be constantly preoccupied with her rear, licking, or scooting along the floor, rug, or grass. The glands may emit an unpleasant odor—similar to a skunk odor.

Blocked anal glands are painful and can become infected. But these glands are rather difficult to empty if you are not familiar with the breed and their exact location. And, if they are indeed blocked, the dog will not be too happy to have you try and try again! Best to let your veterinarian deal with them.

Cysts

You may discover a cyst—a dome-shaped swelling under the skin—while you are petting or grooming your dog. Many older dogs develop these. It does not mean that your dog has cancer!

When to Call the Veterinarian

Go to the vet right away or take your dog to an emergency veterinary clinic if:
- Your dog is choking
- Your dog is having trouble breathing
- Your dog has been injured and you cannot stop the bleeding within a few minutes
- Your dog has been stung or bitten by an insect and the site is swelling
- Your dog has been bitten by a snake
- Your dog has been bitten by another animal (including a dog) and shows any swelling or bleeding
- Your dog has touched, licked, or in any way been exposed to a poison
- Your dog has been burned by either heat or caustic chemicals
- Your dog has been hit by a car
- Your dog has any obvious broken bones or cannot put any weight on one of her limbs
- Your dog has a seizure

Make an appointment to see the vet as soon as possible if:
- Your dog has been bitten by a cat, another dog, or a wild animal
- Your dog has been injured and is still limping an hour later

If you find a cyst on your dog, have your veterinarian check it, just to be sure. He will then advise you about whether it should be watched to see if it grows any larger, or if it should be biopsied and possibly removed.

Diarrhea

Diarrhea can be caused by a sudden change in diet, parasites, digestive upset, or they could be a sign of something serious. The loose, runny stools may or may not contain blood and/or mucus. Other signs of diarrhea may include sporadic, uncontrolled bowel movements.

If diarrhea is not accompanied by any other symptoms, is not uncontrolled, and is not continuous, treat with Imodium A-D liquid. Check with your veterinarian about the dosage. Feed the dog a bland diet of boiled rice and boiled

- Your dog has unexplained swelling or redness
- Your dog's appetite changes
- Your dog vomits repeatedly and can't seem to keep food down, or drools excessively while eating
- You see any changes in your dog's urination or defecation (pain during elimination, change in regular habits, blood in urine or stool, diarrhea, foul-smelling stool)
- Your dog scoots her rear end on the floor
- Your dog's energy level, attitude, or behavior changes for no apparent reason
- Your dog has crusty or cloudy eyes, or excessive tearing or discharge
- Your dog's nose is dry or chapped, hot, crusty, or runny
- Your dog's ears smell foul, have a dark discharge, or seem excessively waxy
- Your dog's gums are inflamed or bleeding, her teeth look brown, or her breath is foul
- Your dog's skin is red, flaky, itchy, or inflamed, or she keeps chewing at certain spots
- Your dog's coat is dull, dry, brittle, or bare in spots
- Your dog's paws are red, swollen, tender, cracked, or the nails are split or too long
- Your dog is panting excessively, wheezing, unable to catch her breath, breathing heavily or sounds strange when she breathes

chopped meat (just a small amount to flavor the rice, and drain off any grease). If the condition persists more than twenty-four hours, seek veterinary care.

Problems of the Genitals

The Dachshund is low to the ground, and therefore the females in particular can sometimes pick up urinary infections. Excess licking of the genitals, excessive urinating, repeated unsuccessful attempts to urinate, and blood in the urine are all signs of such an infection. If the dog is paper trained, small crystals may be visible when urine is dried. Bring a urine sample to the veterinarian, who will use it to determine the proper course of antibiotics.

Males can get infections from licking, which causes pus to form in the sheath of the penis. This condition requires prompt veterinary attention.

Lameness

Lameness—limping, not putting weight on a foot, or favoring one paw—can be caused by many things. Before you do anything, check your dog's paws, including between her toes. There may be burrs or pieces of pinecones, which are sticky and get lodged in the pads and between toes. Carefully remove these with tweezers. If there is a cut and it is not bleeding profusely, apply pressure until the bleeding stops, then put a gauze pad on the foot. If you know from the start that the injury looks serious and the bleeding is profuse, go immediately to your veterinarian.

If the dog has pulled out a toenail, which sometimes happens, this is very painful and you need to make sure it isn't dragging or hanging. It is best to have your veterinarian look at it. Lameness can also result if one or more of her nails are curling under. A veterinarian should handle the trimming of nails that long.

Also, if your dog has jumped down from the furniture, she may have pulled or sprained her shoulders or hurt her leg. Crate rest is best for this. If the pain really bothers her, call your veterinarian and ask what you can give the dog to alleviate her pain. He may want you to bring the dog in if it still bothers her so he can take X-rays to determine the best course of treatment.

It goes without saying that you should never walk your Dachshund on hot pavement. This is not good for the pads of her feet, and puppies whose pads have not hardened could burn their feet.

Internal Parasites

Roundworms (ascarids) are usually found in puppies, and are transmitted to them from their mother. Signs include a pot belly, dull coat, diarrhea, and vomiting. The worms can be seen by the naked eye; they are long, thin, and continuous, resembling spaghetti. Take a stool sample with the worms to your veterinarian. He will dispense the proper medication.

Tapeworms are caused by ingesting fleas, eating animal droppings (rabbits, infested dogs, etc.), and eating dirt contaminated with animal droppings. Signs include constant hunger even though the dog is eating well, no weight gain despite the amount of food eaten, and mucus and sometimes blood in the stool. The worms can be seen with the naked eye. They are long, white, flat, and ribbonlike. Often the first sign will be small, ricelike segments moving about the hair around the anus or on the outer surface of the feces. Take a stool sample with or without the worms to the veterinarian for confirmation. He will dispense the proper medication.

Hookworms live in the small intestines. They attach themselves to intestinal lining and suck blood, causing anemia. These worms cannot be seen with the naked eye. Signs include a general malaise caused by the anemia. Take a stool sample to the veterinarian, who will dispense the proper medication.

Why Spay and Neuter?

Breeding dogs is a serious undertaking that should only be part of a well-planned breeding program. Why? Because dogs pass on their physical and behavioral problems to their offspring. Even healthy, well-behaved dogs can pass on problems in their genes.

Is your dog so sweet that you'd like to have a litter of puppies just like her? If you breed her to another dog, the pups will not have the same genetic heritage she has. Breeding her *parents* again will increase the odds of a similar pup, but even then, the puppies in the second litter could inherit different genes. In fact, *there is no way to breed a dog to be just like another dog*.

Meanwhile, thousands and thousands of dogs are killed in animal shelters every year simply because they have no homes. Casual breeding is a big contributor to this problem.

If you don't plan to breed your dog, is it still a good idea to spay her or neuter him? Yes!

When you spay your female:

- You avoid her heat cycles, during which she discharges blood and scent.
- It greatly reduces the risk of mammary cancer and eliminates the risk of pyometra (an often fatal infection of the uterus) and uterine cancer.
- It prevents unwanted pregnancies.
- It reduces dominance behaviors and aggression.

When you neuter your male:

- It curbs the desire to roam and to fight with other males.
- It greatly reduces the risk of prostate cancer and eliminates the risk of testicular cancer.
- It helps reduce leg lifting and mounting behavior.
- It reduces dominance behaviors and aggression.

Vaccines

What vaccines dogs need and how often they need them has been a subject of controversy for several years. Researchers, health care professionals, vaccine manufacturers, and dog owners do not always agree on which vaccines each dog needs or how often booster shots must be given.

In 2003, the American Animal Hospital Association released vaccination guidelines and recommendations that have helped dog owners and veterinarians sort through much of the controversy and conflicting information. The guidelines designate four vaccines as core, or essential, because of the serious nature of the diseases and their widespread distribution. These are canine distemper virus, canine parvovirus, canine adenovirus-2, and rabies. The general recommendations for their use (except rabies, for which you must follow local laws) are:

- Vaccinate puppies at 6–8 weeks, 9–11 weeks, and 12–14 weeks.
- Give a booster shot when the dog is 1 year old.
- Give a subsequent booster shot every three years, unless there are risk factors that make it necessary to vaccinate more or less often.

Whipworms live in the large intestine and cannot be seen by the naked eye. An infested dog will often have diarrhea that contains blood or mucus. Have a stool sample examined by a veterinarian, who will dispense the proper medication.

Since neither whipworms nor hookworms can be seen with the naked eye, it is best to have a stool check done every six months, especially if your dog is walked or exercised where other dogs have access.

Protozoal parasites include coccidia and giardia, both of which can cause vomiting and diarrhea. Both require veterinary treatment. A vaccine for giardia has recently become available, but is recommended only for dogs with high risk of exposure to the parasite. Check with your veterinarian to see if your Dachshund fits into this category.

Noncore vaccines should only be considered for those dogs who risk exposure to a particular disease because of geographic area, lifestyle, frequency of travel, or other issues. They include vaccines against distemper-measles virus, canine parainfluenza virus, leptospirosis, Bordetella bronchiseptica, and Borrelia burgdorferi (Lyme disease).

Vaccines that are not generally recommended because the disease poses little risk to dogs or is easily treatable, or the vaccine has not been proven to be effective, are those against Giardia, canine coronavirus, and canine adenovirus-1.

Often, combination injections are given to puppies, with one shot containing several core and noncore vaccines. Your veterinarian may be reluctant to use separate shots that do not include the noncore vaccines, because they must be specially ordered. Keep in mind that many vaccines have the potential to produce an allergic reaction, which can be serious in certain individuals. When in doubt about any of these issues, the best advice is to talk things over with your veterinarian.

Heartworm

Heartworm is transmitted by a mosquito that has bitten an infected dog and then bites your dog. The worm larvae travel through the bloodstream and end up in the dog's heart. It can only be diagnosed with a blood test. Dachshunds who live in the warmer parts of the country are at greater risk for contracting heartworms. Symptoms include breathing difficulties, cough, abdominal fluid retention, lethargy, exercise intolerance, and loss of weight despite a good appetite.

This is a life-threatening disease. Treatment can be dangerous and expensive. Prevention is a much better way to deal with heartworm; preventive medications are available. Your veterinarian will advise you as to the best procedure for your dog.

Part III
Enjoying Your Dachshund

Chapter 9

Training Your Dachshund

by Peggy Moran

Training makes your best friend better! A properly trained dog has a happier life and a longer life expectancy. He is also more appreciated by the people he encounters each day, both at home and out and about.

A trained dog walks nicely and joins his family often, going places untrained dogs cannot go. He is never rude or unruly, and he always happily comes when called. When he meets people for the first time, he greets them by sitting and waiting to be petted, rather than jumping up. At home he doesn't compete with his human family, and alone he is not destructive or overly anxious. He isn't continually nagged with words like "no," since he has learned not to misbehave in the first place. He is never shamed, harshly punished, or treated unkindly, and he is a well-loved, involved member of the family.

Sounds good, doesn't it? If you are willing to invest some time, thought, and patience, the words above could soon be used to describe your dog (though perhaps changing "he" to "she"). Educating your pet in a positive way is fun and easy, and there is no better gift you can give your pet than the guarantee of improved understanding and a great relationship.

This chapter will explain how to offer kind leadership, reshape your pet's behavior in a positive and practical way, and even get a head start on simple obedience training.

Understanding Builds the Bond

Dog training is a learning adventure on both ends of the leash. Before attempting to teach their dog new behaviors or change unwanted ones, thoughtful dog owners take the time to understand why their pets behave the way they do, and how their own behavior can be either a positive or negative influence on their dog.

Canine Nature

Loving dogs as much as we do, it's easy to forget they are a completely different species. Despite sharing our homes and living as appreciated members of our families, dogs do not think or learn exactly the same way people do. Even if you love your dog like a child, you must remember to respect the fact that he is actually a dog.

Dogs have no idea when their behavior is inappropriate from a human perspective. They are not aware of the value of possessions they chew or of messes they make or the worry they sometimes seem to cause. While people tend to look at behavior as good and bad or right and wrong, dogs just discover what works and what doesn't work. Then they behave accordingly, learning from their own experiences and increasing or reducing behaviors to improve results for themselves.

You might wonder, "But don't dogs want to please us"? My answer is yes, provided your pleasure reflects back to them in positive ways they can feel and appreciate. Dogs do things for *dog* reasons, and everything they do works for them in some way or they wouldn't be doing it!

The Social Dog

Our pets descended from animals who lived in tightly knit, cooperative social groups. Though far removed in appearance and lifestyle from their ancestors, our dogs still relate in many of the same ways their wild relatives did. And in their relationships with one another, wild canids either lead or follow.

Canine ranking relationships are not about cruelty and power; they are about achievement and abilities. Competent dogs with high levels of drive and confidence step up, while deferring dogs step aside. But followers don't get the short end of the stick; they benefit from the security of having a more competent dog at the helm.

Our domestic dogs still measure themselves against other members of their group—us! Dog owners whose actions lead to positive results have willing, secure followers. But dogs may step up and fill the void or cut loose and do their own thing when their people fail to show capable leadership. When dogs are pushy, aggressive, and rude, or independent and unwilling, it's not because they have designs on the role of "master." It is more likely their owners failed to provide consistent leadership.

Dogs in training benefit from their handler's good leadership. Their education flows smoothly because they are impressed. Being in charge doesn't require you to physically dominate or punish your dog. You simply need to make some subtle changes in the way you relate to him every day.

Lead Your Pack!

Create schedules and structure daily activities. Dogs are creatures of habit and routines will create security. Feed meals at the same times each day and also try to schedule regular walks, training practices, and toilet outings. Your predictability will help your dog be patient.

Ask your dog to perform a task. Before releasing him to food or freedom, have him do something as simple as sit on command. Teach him that cooperation earns great results!

Give a release prompt (such as "let's go") when going through doors leading outside. This is a better idea than allowing your impatient pup to rush past you.

Pet your dog when he is calm, not when he is excited. Turn your touch into a tool that relaxes and settles.

Reward desirable rather than inappropriate behavior. Petting a jumping dog (who hasn't been invited up) reinforces jumping. Pet sitting dogs, and only invite lap dogs up after they've first "asked" by waiting for your invitation.

Replace personal punishment with positive reinforcement. Show a dog what *to do,* and motivate him to want to do it, and there will be no need to punish him for what he should *not do.* Dogs naturally follow, without the need for force or harshness.

Play creatively and appropriately. Your dog will learn the most about his social rank when he is playing with you. During play, dogs work to control toys and try to get the best of one another in a friendly way. The wrong sorts of play can create problems: For example, tug of war can lead to aggressiveness. Allowing your dog to control toys during play may result in possessive guarding when he has something he really values, such as a bone. Dogs who are chased during play may later run away from you when you approach to leash them. The right kinds of play will help increase your dog's social confidence while you gently assert your leadership.

How Dogs Learn (and How They Don't)

Dog training begins as a meeting of minds—yours and your dog's. Though the end goal may be to get your dog's body to behave in a specific way, training starts as a mind game. Your dog is learning all the time by observing the consequences of his actions and social interactions. He is always seeking out what he perceives as desirable and trying to avoid what he perceives as undesirable.

He will naturally repeat a behavior that either brings him more good stuff or makes bad stuff go away (these are both types of reinforcement). He will naturally avoid a behavior that brings him more bad stuff or makes the good stuff go away (these are both types of punishment).

Both reinforcement and punishment can be perceived as either the direct result of something the dog did himself, or as coming from an outside source.

Using Life's Rewards

Your best friend is smart and he is also cooperative. When the best things in life can only be had by working with you, your dog will view you as a facilitator. You unlock doors to all of the positively reinforcing experiences he values: his freedom, his friends at the park, food, affection, walks, and play. The trained dog accompanies you through those doors and waits to see what working with you will bring.

Rewarding your dog for good behavior is called positive reinforcement, and, as we've just seen, it increases the likelihood that he will repeat that behavior. The perfect reward is anything your dog wants that is safe and appropriate. Don't limit yourself to toys, treats, and things that come directly from you. Harness life's positives—barking at squirrels, chasing a falling leaf, bounding away from you at the dog park, pausing for a moment to sniff everything—and allow your dog to earn access to those things as rewards that come from cooperating with you. When he looks at you, when he sits, when he comes when you call—any prompted behavior can earn one of life's rewards. When he works with you, he earns the things he most appreciates; but when he tries to get those things on his own, he cannot. Rather than seeing you as someone who always says "no," your dog will view you as the one who says "let's go!" He will *want* to follow.

What About Punishment?

Not only is it unnecessary to personally punish dogs, it is abusive. No matter how convinced you are that your dog "knows right from wrong," in reality he will associate personal punishment with the punisher. The resulting cowering, "guilty"-looking postures are actually displays of submission and fear. Later,

Purely Positive Reinforcement

With positive training, we emphasize teaching dogs what they should do to earn reinforcements, rather than punishing them for unwanted behaviors.

- Focus on teaching "do" rather than "don't." For example, a sitting dog isn't jumping.
- Use positive reinforcers that are valuable to your dog and the situation: A tired dog values rest; a confined dog values freedom.
- Play (appropriately)!
- Be a consistent leader.
- Set your dog up for success by anticipating and preventing problems.
- Notice and reward desirable behavior, and give him lots of attention when he is being good.
- Train ethically. Use humane methods and equipment that do not frighten or hurt your dog.
- When you are angry, walk away and plan a positive strategy.
- Keep practice sessions short and sweet. Five to ten minutes, three to five times a day is best.

when the punisher isn't around and the coast is clear, the same behavior he was punished for—such as raiding a trash can—might bring a self-delivered, very tasty result. The punished dog hasn't learned not to misbehave; he has learned to not get caught.

Does punishment ever have a place in dog training? Many people will heartily insist it does not. But dog owners often get frustrated as they try to stick to the path of all-positive reinforcement. It sure sounds great, but is it realistic, or even natural, to *never* say "no" to your dog?

A wild dog's life is not *all* positive. Hunger and thirst are both examples of negative reinforcement; the resulting discomfort motivates the wild dog to seek food and water. He encounters natural aversives such as pesky insects; mats in his coat; cold days; rainy days; sweltering hot days; and occasional run-ins with thorns, brambles, skunks, bees, and other nastiness. These all affect his behavior, as he tries to avoid the bad stuff whenever possible. The wild dog also occasionally encounters social punishers from others in his group when he gets too pushy. Starting with a growl or a snap from Mom, and later some mild and ritualized discipline from other members of his four-legged family, he learns to modify behaviors that elicit grouchy responses.

Our pet dogs don't naturally experience all positive results either, because they learn from their surroundings and from social experiences with other dogs. Watch a group of pet dogs playing together and you'll see a very old educational system still being used. As they wrestle and attempt to assert themselves, you'll notice many mouth-on-neck moments. Their playful biting is inhibited, with no intention to cause harm, but their message is clear: "Say uncle or this could hurt more!"

Observing that punishment does occur in nature, some people may feel compelled to try to be like the big wolf with their pet dogs. Becoming aggressive or heavy-handed with your pet will backfire! Your dog will not be impressed, nor will he want to follow you. Punishment causes dogs to change their behavior to avoid or escape discomfort and threats. Threatened dogs will either become very passive and offer submissive, appeasing postures, attempt to flee, or rise to the occasion and fight back. When people personally punish their dogs in an angry manner, one of these three defensive mechanisms will be triggered. Which one depends on a dog's genetic temperament as well as his past social experiences. Since we don't want to make our pets feel the need to avoid or escape us, personal punishment has no place in our training.

Remote Consequences

Sometimes, however, all-positive reinforcement is just not enough. That's because not all reinforcement comes from us. An inappropriate behavior can be self-reinforcing—just doing it makes the dog feel better in some way, whether you are there to say "good boy!" or not. Some examples are eating garbage, pulling the stuffing out of your sofa, barking at passersby, or urinating on the floor.

Although you don't want to personally punish your dog, the occasional deterrent may be called for to help derail these kinds of self-rewarding misbehaviors. In these cases, mild forms of impersonal or remote punishment can be used as part of a correction. The goal isn't to make your dog feel bad or to "know he has done wrong," but to help redirect him to alternate behaviors that are more acceptable to you.

The Problems with Personal Punishment

- Personally punished dogs are not taught appropriate behaviors.
- Personally punished dogs only stop misbehaving when they are caught or interrupted, but they don't learn not to misbehave when they are alone.
- Personally punished dogs become shy, fearful, and distrusting.
- Personally punished dogs may become defensively aggressive.
- Personally punished dogs become suppressed and inhibited.
- Personally punished dogs become stressed, triggering stress-reducing behaviors that their owners interpret as acts of spite, triggering even more punishment.
- Personally punished dogs have stressed owners.
- Personally punished dogs may begin to repeat behaviors they have been taught will result in negative, but predictable, attention.
- Personally punished dogs are more likely to be given away than are positively trained dogs.

You do this by pairing a slightly startling, totally impersonal sound with an equally impersonal and *very mild* remote consequence. The impersonal sound might be a single shake of an empty plastic pop bottle with pennies in it, held out of your dog's sight. Or you could use a vocal expression such as "eh!" delivered with you looking *away* from your misbehaving dog.

Pair your chosen sound—the penny bottle or "eh!"—with either a slight tug on his collar or a sneaky spritz on the rump from a water bottle. Do this right *as* he touches something he should not; bad timing will confuse your dog and undermine your training success.

To keep things under your control and make sure you get the timing right, it's best to do this as a setup. "Accidentally" drop a shoe on the floor, and then help your dog learn some things are best avoided. As he sniffs the shoe say "eh!" without looking at him and give a *slight* tug against his collar. This sound will quickly become meaningful as a correction all by itself—sometimes after just one setup—making the tug correction obsolete. The tug lets your dog see that you were right; going for that shoe *was* a bad idea! Your wise dog will be more likely to heed your warning next time, and probably move closer to you where it's safe. Be a good friend and pick up the nasty shoe. He'll be relieved and you'll look heroic. Later, when he's home alone and encounters a stray shoe, he'll want to give it a wide berth.

Your negative marking sound will come in handy in the future, when your dog begins to venture down the wrong behavioral path. The goal is not to announce your disapproval or to threaten your dog. You are not telling him to stop or showing how *you* feel about his behavior. You are sounding a warning to a friend who's venturing off toward danger—"I wouldn't if I were you!" Suddenly, there is an abrupt, rather startling, noise! Now is the moment to redirect him and help him earn positive reinforcement. That interrupted behavior will become something he wants to avoid in the future, but he won't want to avoid you.

Practical Commands for Family Pets

Before you begin training your dog, let's look at some equipment you'll want to have on hand:

- **A buckle collar** is fine for most dogs. If your dog pulls *very* hard, try a head collar, a device similar to a horse halter that helps reduce pulling by turning the dog's head. *Do not* use a choke chain (sometimes called a training collar), because they cause physical harm even when used correctly.
- **Six-foot training leash and twenty-six–foot retractable leash.**
- **A few empty plastic soda bottles with about twenty pennies in each one.** This will be used to impersonally interrupt misbehaviors before redirecting dogs to more positive activities.
- **A favorite squeaky toy,** to motivate, attract attention, and reward your dog during training.

Lure your dog to take just a few steps with you on the leash by being inviting and enthusiastic. Make sure you reward him for his efforts.

Baby Steps

Allow your young pup to drag a short, lightweight leash attached to a buckle collar for a few *supervised* moments, several times each day. At first the leash may annoy him and he may jump around a bit trying to get away from it. Distract him with your squeaky toy or a bit of his kibble and he'll quickly get used to his new "tail."

Begin walking him on the leash by holding the end and following him. As he adapts, you can begin to assert gentle direct pressure to teach him to follow you. Don't jerk or yank, or he will become afraid to walk when the leash is on. If he becomes hesitant, squat down facing him and let him figure out that by moving toward you he is safe and secure. If he remains confused or frightened and doesn't come to you, go to him and help him understand that you provide safe harbor while he's on the leash. Then back away a few steps and try again to lure him to you. As he learns that you are the "home base," he'll want to follow when you walk a few steps, waiting for you to stop, squat down, and make him feel great.

So Attached to You!

The next step in training your dog—and this is a very important one—is to begin spending at least an hour or more each day with him on a four- to six-foot leash, held by or tethered to you. This training will increase his attachment to you—literally!—as you sit quietly or walk about, tending to your household business. When you are quiet, he'll learn it is time to settle; when you are active, he'll learn to move with you. Tethering also keeps him out of trouble when you are busy but still want his company. It is a great alternative to confining a dog, and can be used instead of crating any time you're home and need to slow him down a bit.

Rotating your dog from supervised freedom to tethered time to some quiet time in the crate or his gated area gives him a diverse and balanced day while he is learning. Two confined or tethered hours is the most you should require of your dog in one stretch, before changing to some supervised freedom, play, or a walk.

The dog in training may, at times, be stressed by all of the changes he is dealing with. Provide a stress outlet, such as a toy to chew on, when he is confined or tethered. He will settle into his quiet time more quickly and completely. Always be sure to provide several rounds of daily play and free time (in a fenced area or on your retractable leash) in addition to plenty of chewing materials.

Dog Talk

Dogs don't speak in words, but they do have a language—body language. They use postures, vocalizations, movements, facial gestures,

Tethering your dog is great way to keep him calm and under control, but still with you.

odors, and touch—usually with their mouths—to communicate what they are feeling and thinking.

We also "speak" using body language. We have quite an array of postures, movements, and facial gestures that accompany our touch and language as we attempt to communicate with our pets. And our dogs can quickly figure us out!

Alone, without associations, words are just noises. But, because we pair them with meaningful body language, our dogs make the connection. Dogs can really learn to understand much of what we *say,* if what we *do* at the same time is consistent.

The Positive Marker

Start your dog's education with one of the best tricks in dog training: Pair various positive reinforcers—food, a toy, touch—with a sound such as a click on a clicker (which you can get at the pet supply store) or a spoken word like "good!" or "yes!" This will enable you to later "mark" your dog's desirable behaviors.

It seems too easy: Just say "yes!" and give the dog his toy. (Or use whatever sound and reward you have chosen.) Later, when you make your marking sound right at the instant your dog does the right thing, he will know you are going to be giving him something good for that particular action. And he'll be eager to repeat the behavior to hear you mark it again!

Next, you must teach your dog to understand the meaning of cues you'll be using to ask him to perform specific behaviors. This is easy, too. Does he already do things you might like him to do on command? Of course! He lies down, he sits, he picks things up, he drops them again, he comes to you. All of the behaviors you'd like to control are already part of your dog's natural repertoire. The trick is getting him to offer those behaviors when you ask for them. And that means you have to teach him to associate a particular behavior on his part with a particular behavior on your part.

Sit Happens

Teach your dog an important new rule: From now on, he is only touched and petted when he is either sitting or lying down. You won't need to ask him to sit; in fact, you should not. Just keeping him tethered near you so there isn't much to do but stand, be ignored, or settle, and wait until sit happens.

He may pester you a bit, but be stoic and unresponsive. Starting now, when *you* are sitting down, a sitting dog is the only one you see and pay attention to. He will eventually sit, and as he does, attach the word "sit"—but don't be too excited or he'll jump right back up. Now mark with your positive sound that promises something good, then reward him with a slow, quiet, settling pet.

Training requires consistent reinforcement. Ask others to also wait until your dog is sitting and calm to touch him, and he will associate being petted with being relaxed. Be sure you train your dog to associate everyone's touch with quiet bonding.

Reinforcing "Sit" as a Command

Since your dog now understands one concept of working for a living—sit to earn petting—you can begin to shape and reinforce his desire to sit. Hold toys, treats, his bowl of food, and turn into a statue. But don't prompt him to sit! Instead, remain frozen and unavailable, looking somewhere out into space, over his head. He will put on a bit of a show, trying to get a response from you, and may offer various behaviors, but only one will push your button—sitting. Wait for him to offer the "right" behavior, and when he does, you unfreeze. Say "sit," then mark with an excited "good!" and give him the toy or treat with a release command—"OK!"

When you notice spontaneous sits occurring, be sure to take advantage of those free opportunities to make your command sequence meaningful and positive. Say "sit" as you observe sit happen—then mark with "good!" and praise, pet, or reward the dog. Soon, every time you look at your dog he'll be sitting and looking right back at you!

Now, after thirty days of purely positive practice, it's time to give him a test. When he is just walking around doing his own thing, suddenly ask him to sit. He'll probably do it right away. If he doesn't, do *not* repeat your command, or you'll just undermine its meaning ("sit" means sit *now;* the command is not "sit, sit, sit, sit"). Instead, get something he likes and let him know you have it. Wait for him to offer the sit—he will—then say "sit!" and complete your marking and rewarding sequence.

OK

"OK" will probably rate as one of your dog's favorite words. It's like the word "recess" to schoolchildren. It is the word used to release your dog from a command. You can introduce "OK" during your "sit" practice. When he gets up from a sit, say "OK" to tell him the sitting is finished. Soon that sound will mean "freedom."

Make it even more meaningful and positive. Whenever he spontaneously bounds away, say "OK!" Squeak a toy, and when he notices and shows interest, toss it for him.

Down

I've mentioned that you should only pet your dog when he is either sitting or lying down. Now, using the approach I've just introduced for "sit," teach your dog to lie down. You will be a statue, and hold something he would like to get but that you'll only release to a dog who is lying down. It helps to lower the desired item to the floor in front of him, still not speaking and not letting him have it until he offers you the new behavior you are seeking.

Lower your dog's reward to the floor to help him figure out what behavior will earn him his reward.

He may offer a sit and then wait expectantly, but you must make him keep searching for the new trick that triggers your generosity. Allow your dog to experiment and find the right answer, even if he has to search around for it first. When he lands on "down" and learns it is another behavior that works, he'll offer it more quickly the next time.

Don't say "down" until he lies down, to tightly associate your prompt with the correct behavior. To say "down, down, down" as he is sitting, looking at you, or pawing at the toy would make "down" mean those behaviors instead! Whichever behavior he offers, a training opportunity has been created. Once you've attached and shaped both sitting and lying down, you can ask for both behaviors with your verbal prompts, "sit" or "down." Be sure to only reinforce the "correct" reply!

Stay

"Stay" can easily be taught as an extension of what you've already been practicing. To teach "stay," you follow the entire sequence for reinforcing a "sit" or "down," except you wait a bit longer before you give the release word, "OK!" Wait a second or two longer during each practice before saying "OK!" and releasing your dog to the positive reinforcer (toy, treat, or one of life's other rewards).

You can step on the leash to help your dog understand the down-stay, but only do this when he is already lying down. You don't want to hurt him!

If he gets up before you've said "OK," you have two choices: pretend the release was your idea and quickly interject "OK!" as he breaks; or, if he is more experienced and practiced, mark the behavior with your correction sound—"eh!"— and then gently put him back on the spot, wait for him to lie down, and begin again. Be sure the next three practices are a success. Ask him to wait for just a second, and release him before he can be wrong. You need to keep your dog feeling like more of a success than a failure as you begin to test his training in increasingly more distracting and difficult situations.

As he gets the hang of it—he stays until you say "OK"— you can gradually push for longer times—up to a minute on a sit-stay, and up to three minutes on a down-stay. You can also gradually add distractions and work in new environments. To add a minor self-correction for the down-stay, stand on the dog's leash after he lies down, allowing about three inches of slack. If tries to get up before you've said "OK," he'll discover it doesn't work.

Do not step on the leash to make your dog lie down! This could badly hurt his neck, and will destroy his trust in you. Remember, we are teaching our dogs to make the best choices, not inflicting our answers upon them!

Come

Rather than thinking of "come" as an action—"come to me"—think of it as a place—"the dog is sitting in front of me, facing me." Since your dog by now really likes sitting to earn your touch and other positive reinforcement, he's likely to sometimes sit directly in front of you, facing you, all on his own. When this happens, give it a specific name: "come."

Now follow the rest of the training steps you have learned to make him like doing it and reinforce the behavior by practicing it any chance you get. Anything your dog wants and likes could be earned as a result of his first offering the sit-in-front known as "come."

You can help guide him into the right location. Use your hands as "landing gear" and pat the insides of your legs at his nose level. Do this while backing up a bit, to help him maneuver to the straight-in-front, facing-you position. Don't say the

Pat the insides of your legs to show your dog exactly where you like him to sit when you say "come."

word "come" while he's maneuvering, because he hasn't! You are trying to make "come" the end result, not the work in progress.

You can also help your dog by marking his movement in the right direction: Use your positive sound or word to promise he is getting warm. When he finally sits facing you, enthusiastically say "come," mark again with your positive word, and release him with an enthusiastic "OK!" Make it so worth his while, with lots of play and praise, that he can't wait for you to ask him to come again!

Building a Better Recall

Practice, practice, practice. Now, practice some more. Teach your dog that all good things in life hinge upon him first sitting in front of you in a behavior named "come." When you think he really has got it, test him by asking him to "come" as you gradually add distractions and change locations. Expect setbacks as you make these changes and practice accordingly. Lower your expectations and make his task easier so he is able to get it right. Use those distractions as rewards, when they are appropriate. For example, let him check out the interesting leaf that blew by as a reward for first coming to you and ignoring it.

Add distance and call your dog to come while he is on his retractable leash. If he refuses and sits looking at you blankly, *do not* jerk, tug, "pop," or reel him in. Do nothing! It is his move; wait to see what behavior he offers. He'll either begin to approach (mark the behavior with an excited "good!"), sit and do nothing (just keep waiting), or he'll try to move in some direction other than toward you. If he tries to leave, use your correction marker—"eh!"—and bring him to a stop by letting him walk to the end of the leash, *not* by jerking him. Now walk to him in a neutral manner, and don't jerk or show any disapproval. Gently bring him back to the spot where he was when you called him, then back away and face him, still waiting and not reissuing your command. Let him keep examining his options until he finds the one that works—yours!

If you have practiced everything I've suggested so far and given your dog a chance to really learn what "come" means, he is well aware of what you want and is quite intelligently weighing all his options. The only way he'll know your way is the one that works is to be allowed to examine his other choices and discover that they *don't* work.

Sooner or later every dog tests his training. Don't be offended or angry when your dog tests you. No matter how positive you've made it, he won't always want to do everything you ask, every time. When he explores the "what happens if I don't" scenario, your training is being strengthened. He will discover through his own process of trial and error that the best—and only—way out of a command he really doesn't feel compelled to obey is to obey it.

Let's Go

Many pet owners wonder if they can retain control while walking their dogs and still allow at least some running in front, sniffing, and playing. You might worry that allowing your dog occasional freedom could result in him expecting it all the time, leading to a testy, leash-straining walk. It's possible for both parties on the leash to have an enjoyable experience by implementing and reinforcing well-thought-out training techniques.

Begin by making word associations you'll use on your walks. Give the dog some slack on the leash, and as he starts to walk away from you say "OK" and begin to follow him.

Do not let him drag you; set the pace even when he is being given a turn at being the leader. Whenever he starts to pull, just come to a standstill and refuse to move (or refuse to allow him to continue forward) until there is slack in the leash. Do this correction without saying anything at all. When he isn't pulling, you may decide to just stand still and let him sniff about within the range the slack leash allows, or you may even mosey along following him. After a few minutes of "recess," it is time to work. Say something like "that's it" or "time's up," close the distance between you and your dog, and touch him.

Next say "let's go" (or whatever command you want to use to mean "follow me as we walk"). Turn and walk off, and, if he follows, mark his behavior with "good!" Then stop,

Give your dog slack on his leash as you walk and let him make the decision to walk with you.

When your dog catches up with you, make sure you let him know what a great dog he is!

Intersperse periods of attentive walking, where your dog is on a shorter leash, with periods on a slack leash, where he is allowed to look and sniff around.

squat down, and let him catch you. Make him glad he did! Start again, and do a few transitions as he gets the hang of your follow-the-leader game, speeding up, slowing down, and trying to make it fun. When you stop, he gets to catch up and receive some deserved positive reinforcement. Don't forget that's the reason he is following you, so be sure to make it worth his while!

Require him to remain attentive to you. Do not allow sniffing, playing, eliminating, or pulling during your time as leader on a walk. If he seems to get distracted—which, by the way, is the main reason dogs walk poorly with their people— change direction or pace without saying a word. Just help him realize "oops, I lost track of my human." Do not jerk his neck and say "heel"—this will make the word "heel" mean pain in the neck and will not encourage him to cooperate with you. Don't repeat "let's go," either. He needs to figure out that it is his job to keep track of and follow you if he wants to earn the positive benefits you provide.

The best reward you can give a dog for performing an attentive, controlled walk is a few minutes of walking without all of the controls. Of course, he must remain on a leash even during the "recess" parts of the walk, but allowing him to discriminate between attentive following—"let's go"—and having a few moments of relaxation—"OK"—will increase his willingness to work.

Training for Attention

Your dog pretty much has a one-track mind. Once he is focused on something, everything else is excluded. This can be great, for instance, when he's focusing on you! But it can also be dangerous if, for example, his attention is riveted on the bunny he is chasing and he does not hear you call—that is, not unless he has been trained to pay attention when you say his name.

When you say your dog's name, you'll want him to make eye contact with you. Begin teaching this by making yourself so intriguing that he can't help but look.

When you call your dog's name, you will again be seeking a specific response—eye contact. The best way to teach this is to trigger his alerting response by making a noise with your mouth, such as whistling or a kissing sound, and then immediately doing something he'll find very intriguing.

You can play a treasure hunt game to help teach him to regard his name as a request for attention. As a bonus, you can reinforce the rest of his new vocabulary at the same time.

Treasure Hunt

Make a kissing sound, then jump up and find a dog toy or dramatically raid the fridge and rather noisily eat a piece of cheese. After doing this twice, make a kissing sound and then look at your dog.

Of course he is looking at you! He is waiting to see if that sound—the kissing sound—means you're going to go hunting again. After all, you're so good at it! Because he is looking, say his name, mark with "good," then go hunting and find his toy. Release it to him with an "OK." At any point if he follows you, attach your "let's go!" command; if he leaves you, give permission with "OK."

Using this approach, he cannot be wrong—any behavior your dog offers can be named. You can add things like "take it" when he picks up a toy, and "thank you" when he happens to drop one. Many opportunities to make your new vocabulary meaningful and positive can be found within this simple training game.

Problems to watch out for when teaching the treasure hunt:

- You really do not want your dog to come to you when you call his name (later, when you try to engage his attention to ask him to stay, he'll already be on his way toward you). You just want him to look at you.
- Saying "watch me, watch me" doesn't teach your dog to *offer* his attention. It just makes you a background noise.
- Don't lure your dog's attention with the reward. Get his attention and then reward him for looking. Try holding a toy in one hand with your arm stretched out to your side. Wait until he looks at you rather than the toy. Now say his name then mark with "good!" and release the toy. As he goes for it, say "OK."

To get your dog's attention, try holding his toy with your arm out to your side. Wait until he looks at you, then mark the moment and give him the toy.

Teaching Cooperation

Never punish your dog for failing to obey you or try to punish him into compliance. Bribing, repeating yourself, and doing a behavior for him all avoid the real issue of dog training—his will. He must be helped to be willing, not made to achieve tasks. Good dog training helps your dog want to obey. He learns that he can gain what he values most through cooperation and compliance, and can't gain those things any other way.

Your dog is learning to *earn,* rather than expect, the good things in life. And you've become much more important to him than you were before. Because you are allowing him to experiment and learn, he doesn't have to be forced, manipulated, or bribed. When he wants something, he can gain it by cooperating with you. One of those "somethings"—and a great reward you shouldn't underestimate—is your positive attention, paid to him with love and sincere approval!

Chapter 10

Housetraining Your Dachshund

Excerpted from Housetraining: An Owner's Guide to
a Happy Healthy Pet, 1st Edition, *by September Morn*

By the time puppies are about 3 weeks old, they start to follow their
mother around. When they are a few steps away from their clean sleeping
area, the mama dog stops. The pups try to nurse but mom won't allow it. The
pups mill around in frustration, then nature calls and they all urinate and defecate here, away from their bed. The mother dog returns to the nest, with her
brood waddling behind her. Their first housetraining lesson has been a success.

The next one to housetrain puppies should be their breeder. The breeder
watches as the puppies eliminate, then deftly removes the soiled papers and
replaces them with clean papers before the pups can traipse back through their
messes. He has wisely arranged the puppies' space so their bed, food, and drinking water are as far away from the elimination area as possible. This way, when
the pups follow their mama, they will move away from their sleeping and eating
area before eliminating. This habit will help the pups be easily housetrained.

Your Housetraining Shopping List

While your puppy's mother and breeder are getting her started on good housetraining habits, you'll need to do some shopping. If you have all the essentials
in place before your dog arrives, it will be easier to help her learn the rules from
day one.

Newspaper: The younger your puppy and larger her breed, the more newspapers you'll need. Newspaper is absorbent, abundant, cheap, and convenient.

Puddle Pads: If you prefer not to stockpile newspaper, a commercial alternative is puddle pads. These thick paper pads can be purchased under several trade names at pet supply stores. The pads have waterproof backing, so puppy urine doesn't seep through onto the floor. Their disadvantages are that they will cost you more than newspapers and that they contain plastics that are not biodegradable.

Poop Removal Tool: There are several types of poop removal tools available. Some are designed with a separate pan and rake, and others have the handles hinged like scissors. Some scoops need two hands for operation, while others are designed for one-handed use. Try out the different brands at your pet supply store. Put a handful of pebbles or dog kibble on the floor and then pick them up with each type of scoop to determine which works best for you.

Plastic Bags: When you take your dog outside your yard, you *must* pick up after her. Dog waste is unsightly, smelly, and can harbor disease. In many cities and towns, the law mandates dog owners clean up pet waste deposited on public ground. Picking up after your dog using a plastic bag scoop is simple. Just put your hand inside the bag, like a mitten, and then grab the droppings. Turn the bag inside out, tie the top, and that's that.

Crate: To housetrain a puppy, you will need some way to confine her when you're unable to supervise. A dog crate is a secure way to confine your dog for short periods during the day and to use as a comfortable bed at night. Crates come in wire mesh and in plastic. The wire ones are foldable to store flat in a smaller space. The plastic ones are more cozy, draft-free, and quiet, and are approved for airline travel.

Baby Gates: Since you shouldn't crate a dog for more than an hour or two at a time during the day, baby gates are a good way to limit your dog's freedom in the house. Be sure the baby gates you use are safe. The old-fashioned wooden, expanding lattice type has seriously injured a number of children by collapsing and trapping a leg, arm, or neck. That type of gate can hurt a puppy, too, so use the modern grid type gates instead. You'll need more than one baby gate if you have several doorways to close off.

Exercise Pen: Portable exercise pens are great when you have a young pup or a small dog. These metal or plastic pens are made of rectangular panels that are hinged together. The pens are freestanding, sturdy, foldable, and can be carried like a suitcase. You could set one up in your kitchen as the pup's daytime corral, and then take it outdoors to contain your pup while you garden or just sit and enjoy the day.

Enzymatic Cleaner: All dogs make housetraining mistakes. Accept this and be ready for it by buying an enzymatic cleaner made especially for pet accidents. Dogs like to eliminate where they have done it before, and lingering smells lead them to those spots. Ordinary household cleaners may remove all the odors you can smell, but only an enzymatic cleaner will remove everything your dog can smell.

The First Day

Housetraining is a matter of establishing good habits in your dog. That means you never want her to learn anything she will eventually have to unlearn. Start off housetraining on the right foot by teaching your dog that you prefer her to eliminate outside. Designate a potty area in your backyard (if you have one) or

Your puppy's mom gave her housetraining lessons starting at about 3 weeks old. You can capitalize on those early lessons by reinforcing good habits and never letting her establish bad ones.

in the street in front of your home and take your dog to it as soon as you arrive home. Let her sniff a bit and, when she squats to go, give the action a name: "potty" or "do it" or anything else you won't be embarrassed to say in public. Eventually your dog will associate that word with the act and will eliminate on command. When she's finished, praise her with "good potty!"

That first day, take your puppy out to the potty area frequently. Although she may not eliminate every time, you are establishing a routine: You take her to her spot, ask her to eliminate, and praise her when she does.

Just before bedtime, take your dog to her potty area once more. Stand by and wait until she produces. Do not put your dog to bed for the night until she has eliminated. Be patient and calm. This is not the time to play with or excite your dog. If she's too excited, a pup not only won't eliminate, she probably won't want to sleep either.

Most dogs, even young ones, will not soil their beds if they can avoid it. For this reason, a sleeping crate can be a tremendous help during housetraining. Being crated at night can help a dog develop the muscles that control elimination. So after your dog has emptied out, put her to bed in her crate.

A good place to put your dog's sleeping crate is near your own bed. Dogs are pack animals, so they feel safer sleeping with others in a common area. In your bedroom, the pup will be near you and you'll be close enough to hear when she wakes during the night and needs to eliminate.

Pups under 4 months old often are not able to hold their urine all night. If your puppy has settled down to sleep but awakens and fusses a few hours later, she probably needs to go out. For the best housetraining progress, take your pup to her elimination area whenever she needs to go, even in the wee hours of the morning.

Don't Overuse the Crate

A crate serves well as a dog's overnight bed, but you should not leave the dog in her crate for more than an hour or two during the day. Throughout the day, she needs to play and exercise. She is likely to want to drink some water and will undoubtedly eliminate. Confining your dog all day will give her no option but to soil her crate. This is not just unpleasant for you and the dog, but it reinforces bad cleanliness habits. And crating a pup for the whole day is abusive. Don't do it.

Your pup may soil in her crate if you ignore her late night urgency. It's unfair to let this happen, and it sends the wrong message about your expectations for cleanliness. Resign yourself to this midnight outing and just get up and take the pup out. Your pup will outgrow this need soon and will learn in the process that she can count on you, and you'll wake happily each morning to a clean dog.

The next morning, the very first order of business is to take your pup out to eliminate. Don't forget to take her to her special potty spot, ask her to eliminate, and then praise her when she does. After your pup empties out in the morning, give her breakfast, and then take her to her potty area again. After that, she shouldn't need to eliminate again right away, so you can allow her some free playtime. Keep an eye on the pup though, because when she pauses in play she may need to go potty. Take her to the right spot, give the command, and praise if she produces.

Confine Your Pup

A pup or dog who has not finished housetraining should *never* be allowed the run of the house unattended. A new dog (especially a puppy) with unlimited access to your house will make her own choices about where to eliminate.

Vigilance during your new dog's first few weeks in your home will pay big dividends. Every potty mistake delays housetraining progress; every success speeds it along.

Prevent problems by setting up a controlled environment for your new pet. A good place for a puppy corral is often the kitchen. Kitchens almost always have waterproof or easily cleaned floors, which is a distinct asset with leaky pups. A bathroom, laundry room, or enclosed porch could be used for a puppy corral, but the kitchen is generally

Confinement is one of the most important aspects of housetraining. Unlimited access to the house means unlimited choices about where to eliminate.

the best location. Kitchens are a meeting place and a hub of activity for many families, and a puppy will learn better manners when she is socialized thoroughly with family, friends, and nice strangers.

The way you structure your pup's corral area is very important. Her bed, food, and water should be at the opposite end of the corral from the potty area.

When you first get your pup, spread newspaper over the rest of the floor of her playpen corral. Lay the papers at least four pages thick and be sure to overlap the edges. As you note the pup's progress, you can remove the papers nearest the sleeping and eating corner. Gradually decrease the size of the papered area until only the end where you want the pup to eliminate is covered. If you will be training your dog to eliminate outside, place newspaper at the end of the corral that is closest to the door that leads outdoors. That way as she moves away from the clean area to the papered area, the pup will also form the habit of heading toward the door to go out.

Maintain a scent marker for the pup's potty area by reserving a small soiled piece of paper when you clean up. Place this piece, with her scent of urine, under the top sheet of the clean papers you spread. This will cue your pup where to eliminate.

Most dog owners use a combination of indoor papers and outdoor elimination areas. When the pup is left by herself in the corral, she can potty on the ever-present newspaper. When you are available to take the pup outside, she can do her business in the outdoor spot. It is not difficult to switch a pup from indoor paper training to outdoor elimination. Owners of large pups often switch early, but potty papers are still useful if the pup spends time in her indoor corral while you're away. Use the papers as long as your pup needs them. If you come home and they haven't been soiled, you are ahead.

When setting up your pup's outdoor yard, put the lounging area as far away as possible from the potty area, just as with the indoor corral setup. People with large yards, for example, might leave a patch unmowed at the edge of the lawn to serve as the dog's elimination area. Other dog owners teach the dog to relieve herself in a designated corner of a deck or patio. For an apartment-dwelling city dog, the outdoor potty area might be a tiny balcony or the curb. Each dog owner has somewhat different expectations for their dog. Teach your dog to eliminate in a spot that suits your environment and lifestyle.

> **TIP**
>
> **Water**
>
> Make sure your dog has access to clean water at all times. Limiting the amount of water a dog drinks is not necessary for housetraining success and can be very dangerous. A dog needs water to digest food, to maintain a proper body temperature and proper blood volume, and to clean her system of toxins and wastes. A healthy dog will automatically drink the right amount. Do not restrict water intake. Controlling your dog's access to water is not the key to housetraining her; controlling her access to everything else in your home is.

City dogs will need to learn to eliminate out in the street. It's no problem for your smart Dachshund!

Be sure to pick up droppings in your yard at least once a day. Dogs have a natural desire to stay far away from their own excrement, and if too many piles litter the ground, your dog won't want to walk through it and will start eliminating elsewhere. Leave just one small piece of feces in the potty area to remind your dog where the right spot is located.

To help a pup adapt to the change from indoors to outdoors, take one of her potty papers outside to the new elimination area. Let the pup stand on the paper when she goes potty outdoors. Each day for four days, reduce the size of the paper by half. By the fifth day, the pup, having used a smaller and smaller piece of paper to stand on, will probably just go to that spot and eliminate.

Take your pup to her outdoor potty place frequently throughout the day. A puppy can hold her urine for only about as many hours as her age in months, and will move her bowels as many times a day as she eats. So a 2-month-old pup will urinate about every two hours, while at 4 months she can manage about four hours between piddles. Pups vary somewhat in their rate of development, so this is not a hard and fast rule. It does, however, present a realistic idea of how long a pup can be left without access to a potty place. Past 4 months, her potty trips will be less frequent.

When you take the dog outdoors to her spot, keep her leashed so that she won't wander away. Stand quietly and let her sniff around in the designated area. If your pup starts to leave before she has eliminated, gently lead her back and remind her to go. If your pup sniffs at the spot, praise her calmly, say the command word, and just wait. If she produces, praise serenely, then give her time to

Backyard potty breaks should be all business. Don't let your pup turn them into playtime.

sniff around a little more. She may not be finished, so give her time to go again before allowing her to play and explore her new home.

If you find yourself waiting more than five minutes for your dog to potty, take her back inside. Watch your pup carefully for twenty minutes, not giving her any opportunity to slip away to eliminate unnoticed. If you are too busy to watch the pup, put her in her crate. After twenty minutes, take her to the outdoor potty spot again and tell her what to do. If you're unsuccessful after five minutes, crate the dog again. Give her another chance to eliminate in fifteen or twenty minutes. Eventually, she will have to go.

Watch Your Pup

Be vigilant and don't let the pup make a mistake in the house. Each time you successfully anticipate elimination and take your pup to the potty spot, you'll move a step closer to your goal. Stay aware of your puppy's needs. If you ignore the pup, she will make mistakes and you'll be cleaning up more messes.

Keep a chart of your new dog's elimination behavior for the first three or four days. Jot down what times she eats, sleeps, and eliminates. After several days a pattern will emerge that can help you determine your pup's body rhythms. Most dogs tend to eliminate at fairly regular intervals. Once you know your new dog's natural rhythms, you'll be able to anticipate her needs and schedule appropriate potty outings.

Understanding the meanings of your dog's postures can also help you win the battle of the puddle. When your dog is getting ready to eliminate, she will display a specific set of postures. The sooner you can learn to read these signals, the cleaner your floor will stay.

A young puppy who feels the urge to eliminate may start to sniff the ground and walk in a circle. If the pup is very young, she may simply squat and go. All young puppies, male or female, squat to urinate. If you are housetraining a pup under 4 months of age, regardless of sex, watch for the beginnings of a squat as the signal to rush the pup to the potty area.

When a puppy is getting ready to defecate, she may run urgently back and forth or turn in a circle while sniffing or starting to squat. If defecation is imminent, the pup's anus may protrude or open slightly. When she starts to go, the pup will squat and hunch her back, her tail sticking straight out behind. There is no mistaking this posture; nothing else looks like this. If your pup takes this position, take her to her potty area. Hurry! You may have to carry her to get there in time.

A young puppy won't have much time between feeling the urge and actually eliminating, so you'll have to be quick to note her postural clues and intercept your pup in time. Pups from 3 to 6 months have a few seconds more between the urge and the act than younger ones do. The older your pup, the more time you'll have to get her to the potty area after she begins the posture signals that alert you to her need.

Accidents Happen

If you see your pup about to eliminate somewhere other than the designated area, interrupt her immediately. Say "wait, wait, wait!" or clap your hands loudly to startle her into stopping. Carry the pup, if she's still small enough, or take her collar and lead her to the correct area. Once your dog is in the potty area, give her the command to eliminate. Use a friendly voice for the command, then wait patiently for her to produce. The pup may be tense because you've just startled her and may have to relax a bit before she's able to eliminate. When she does her job, include the command word in the praise you give ("good potty").

The old-fashioned way of housetraining involved punishing a dog's mistakes even before she knew what she was supposed to do. Puppies were punished for breaking rules they didn't understand about functions they couldn't control.

This was not fair. While your dog is new to housetraining, there is no need or excuse for punishing her mistakes. Your job is to take the dog to the potty area just before she needs to go, especially with pups under 3 months old. If you aren't watching your pup closely enough and she has an accident, don't punish the puppy for your failure to anticipate her needs. It's not the pup's fault; it's yours.

In any case, punishment is not an effective tool for housetraining most dogs. Many will react to punishment by hiding puddles and feces where you won't find them right away (like behind the couch or under the desk). This eventually may lead to punishment after the fact, which leads to more hiding, and so on.

Instead of punishing for mistakes, stay a step ahead of potty accidents by learning to anticipate your pup's needs. Accompany your dog to the designated potty area when she needs to go. Tell her what you want her to do and praise her when she goes. This will work wonders. Punishment won't be necessary if you are a good teacher.

What happens if you come upon a mess after the fact? Some trainers say a dog can't remember having eliminated, even a few moments after she has done so. This is not true. The fact is that urine and feces carry a dog's unique scent, which she (and every other dog) can instantly recognize. So, if you happen upon a potty mistake after the fact you can still use it to teach your dog.

Punishing your pup for accidents will only encourage her to be more secretive about where she eliminates.

But remember, no punishment! Spanking, hitting, shaking, or scaring a puppy for having a housetraining accident is confusing and counterproductive. Spend your energy instead on positive forms of teaching.

Instead of punishing your puppy for mistakes, set her up for success by getting her outside on a regular schedule.

Take your pup and a paper towel to the mess. Point to the urine or feces and calmly tell your puppy, "no potty here." Then scoop or sop up the accident with the paper towel. Take the evidence and the pup to the approved potty area. Drop the mess on the ground and tell the dog, "good potty here," as if she had done the deed in the right place. If your pup sniffs at the evidence, praise her calmly. If the accident happened very recently your dog may not have to go yet, but wait with her a few minutes anyway. If she eliminates, praise her. Afterwards, go finish cleaning up the mess.

Soon the puppy will understand that there is a place where you are pleased about elimination and other places where you are not. Praising for elimination in the approved place will help your pup remember the rules.

Scheduling Basics

With a new puppy in the home, don't be surprised if your rising time is suddenly a little earlier than you've been accustomed to. Puppies have earned a reputation as very early risers. When your pup wakes you at the crack of dawn, you will have to get up and take her to her elimination spot. Be patient. When your dog is an adult, she may enjoy sleeping in as much as you do.

At the end of this chapter, you'll find a typical housetraining schedule for puppies aged 10 weeks to 6 months. (To find schedules for younger and older pups, and for adult dogs, visit this book's companion web site.) It's fine to adjust the rising times when using this schedule, but you should not adjust the intervals between feedings and potty outings unless your pup's behavior justifies a change. Your puppy can only meet your expectations in housetraining if you help her learn the rules.

The schedule for puppies is devised with the assumption that someone will be home most of the time with the pup. That would be the best scenario, of course, but is not always possible. You may be able to ease the problems of a latchkey pup by having a neighbor or friend look in on the pup at noon and take her to eliminate. A better solution might be hiring a pet sitter to drop by midday. A professional pet sitter will be knowledgeable about companion animals and can give your pup high-quality care and socialization. Some can even help train your pup in both potty manners and basic obedience. Ask your veterinarian and your dog-owning friends to recommend a good pet sitter.

A reasonable schedule will include time when your puppy can be out and about in the house with you. If she's nearby on a leash, you can watch her for signs that she needs a potty break.

If you must leave your pup alone during her early housetraining period, be sure to cover the entire floor of her corral with thick layers of overlapping newspaper. If you come home to messes in the puppy corral, just clean them up. Be patient—she's still a baby.

Use this schedule (and the ones on the companion web site) as a basic plan to help prevent housetraining accidents. Meanwhile, use your own powers of observation to discover how to best modify the basic schedule to fit your dog's unique needs. Each dog is an individual and will have her own rhythms, and each dog is reliable at a different age.

Schedule for Pups 10 Weeks to 6 Months

7:00 a.m.	Get up and take the puppy from her sleeping crate to her potty spot.
7:15	Clean up last night's messes, if any.
7:30	Food and fresh water.
7:45	Pick up the food bowl. Take the pup to her potty spot; wait and praise.

continues

Schedule for Pups 10 Weeks to 6 Months *(continued)*

8:00	The pup plays around your feet while you have your breakfast.
9:00	Potty break (younger pups may not be able to wait this long).
9:15	Play and obedience practice.
10:00	Potty break.
10:15	The puppy is in her corral with safe toys to chew and play with.
11:30	Potty break (younger pups may not be able to wait this long).
11:45	Food and fresh water.
12:00 p.m.	Pick up the food bowl and take the pup to her potty spot.
12:15	The puppy is in her corral with safe toys to chew and play with.
1:00	Potty break (younger pups may not be able to wait this long).
1:15	Put the pup on a leash and take her around the house with you.
3:30	Potty break (younger pups may not be able to wait this long).
3:45	Put the pup in her corral with safe toys and chews for solitary play and/or a nap.
4:45	Potty break.
5:00	Food and fresh water.
5:15	Potty break.
5:30	The pup may play nearby (either leashed or in her corral) while you prepare your evening meal.
7:00	Potty break.
7:15	Leashed or closely watched, the pup may play and socialize with family and visitors.
9:15	Potty break (younger pups may not be able to wait this long).
10:45	Last chance to potty.
11:00	Put the pup to bed in her crate for the night.

Learning More About Your Dachshund

Some Good Books

About Dachshunds

Adamson, Eve, *Dachshunds For Dummies*, Wiley Publishing, Inc., 2001.

Gordon, Ann, *The Dachshund, A Dog for Town and Country*, Howell Book House, 2000.

Heesom, Elizabeth, *Dachshunds: An Owner's Companion*, Trafalgar Square, 1996.

Care and Health

Carlson, Liisa, DVM, and James Giffin, MD, *Dog Owners Home Veterinary Handbook*, 3rd Edition, Howell Book House, 1999.

Hoffman, Matthew, Editor, *Dogs, the Ultimate Care Guide: Good Health, Loving Care, Maximum Longevity*, Rodale Press, 2000.

Vella, Bob, and Ken Leebow, *300 Incredible Things for Pet Lovers on the Internet*, 300 Incredible.com, 2000.

Volhard, Wendy, and Kerry Brown, DVM, *Holistic Guide for a Healthy Dog*, Howell Book House, 2000.

Training

Benjamin, Carol Lea, *Dog Training in 10 Minutes,* Howell Book House, 1996.

Ross, John, and Barbara McKinney, *Dog Talk: Training Your Dog Through a Canine Point of View,* St. Martin's Press, 1995.

Rutherford, Clarice, and David H. Neil, MRCVS, *How to Raise a Puppy You Can Live With,* Alpine Publications, 1999.

Smith, Cheryl S., *The Rosetta Bone—The Key to Communication Between Humans and Canines,* Howell Book House, 2004.

Volhard, Jack, and Melissa Bartlett, *What All Good Dogs Should Know: The Sensible Way to Train,* Howell Book House, 1991.

Canine Activities

Alston, George, *The Winning Edge: Show Ring Secrets,* Howell Book House, 1992.

Bonham, Margaret H., *Having Fun with Agility,* Howell Book House, 2004.

Burch, Mary R., *Wanted! Animal Volunteers,* Howell Book House, 2002.

Hall, Lynn, *Dog Showing for Beginners,* Howell Book House, 1994.

O'Neil, Jacqueline F., *All About Agility,* Howell Book House, 1999.

Volhard, Jack, and Wendy Volhard, *The Canine Good Citizen: Every Dog Can Be One,* Second Edition, Howell Book House, 1997.

Periodicals

AKC Gazette
American Kennel Club
260 Madison Ave.
New York, NY 10016
(212) 696-8200
www.akc.org

The Bark
2810 8th St.
Berkeley, CA 94710
(510) 704-0827
www.thebark.com

The Dachshund Club of America Newsletter
www.dachshund-dca.org

Dog Fancy
P.O. Box 53264
Boulder, CO 80322-3264
www.dogfancy.com

Dog Watch
P.O. Box 420235
Palm Coast, FL 32142-0235
(800) 829-5574
www.vet.cornell.edu/publicresources/dog.htm#ifo

Index

Photo Credits:

Mary Bloom: 1, 4–5, 8–9, 16, 17, 25, 27, 33, 38, 39, 41, 42, 53, 58, 59, 63, 69, 73, 78, 86, 87, 94, 95, 96, 137
Kent Dannen: 11, 13, 14, 19, 20, 22, 26, 28, 30, 31, 32, 34, 36, 37, 40, 45, 46, 47, 49, 50–51, 52, 61, 62, 67, 68, 70, 71, 74, 76, 79, 83, 89, 91, 104–105, 106, 126, 128, 130, 132, 133, 135, 136